"Do you ever feel inadequate to be used by God? Insecure? Unsure of yourself? If so, Adam's new book *Talking with God* will build your faith in the power of God. If you want to strengthen your daily prayer life, grab this book!"

—CRAIG GROESCHEL, pastor of Life.Church and author
of *Divine Direction*

"Adam is a friend and a great leader who loves Jesus. I mean loves Jesus with everything in him. Seeing Adam's faith and relationship with Jesus expressed in a book on simple prayer, has me all in! I'll be giving a copy to everyone on my team at Catalyst because I think it's that important to read!"

—TYLER REAGIN, executive director of CATALYST

"I love this book because I love the author! Adam is so easy to talk with and in the pages you are about to turn, he'll help you realize that talking with God is easy too. Accessible. Practical. Biblical. This is a must-read!"

—JON WEECE, author of *Me Too*

"We cannot thrive without the depth and intimacy of prayer that Adam describes in a beautifully simplistic way. *Talking with God* is both refreshing and insightful. This is a book we all need to read."

—JARRID WILSON, pastor and author of *Love Is Oxygen*

"It's been said that 'prayer is to the soul what breathing is to the body.' If that's true, most of us are spiritually asthmatic. In this delightful book, Adam Weber offers a bit of spiritual 'respiratory therapy.' *Talking with God* is disarming, helpful, and inspiring. It will leave you wanting to pursue a deeper and more regular prayer life."

—ADAM HAMILTON, pastor and author of *Creed*

"Prayer has always been a place of connection for me but also a place of some confusion, if I'm honest. Adam does an incredible job of walking us through what it means to have a conversation with God, to talk and to listen, and to embrace the mystery that comes with it."

—ANNIE F. DOWNS, author of *Let's All Be Brave*

"*Talking with God* is a book on prayer for prodigals and the imperfect. Adam speaks on prayer not as someone who has it all figured out but rather as someone who's on the journey. He reminds us that regardless of who we are or where we've been, we can talk with God."

—MIKE FOSTER, author of *People of the Second Chance*

"This book on prayer will be an answer to prayer for many. Adam is a guy who loves people and loves helping them navigate difficulties and messes of life to connect to what really matters. We've overcomplicated communicating with the God who made us and loves us. This book is a gust of encouragement that will reconnect you to what really matters in this life. It's been a gift to me, and I hope this book finds its way into the hands of anyone else looking for a true lift."

—BRAD MONTAGUE, creator of Kid President

"I've known Adam for years. He understands that in order to truly make a difference in this life, he, along with you and I need to be in constant conversation with Jesus, the One who is able to change everything. This is a book on prayer for those who intend to change the world but are aware they can't do it on their own."

—BRAD LOMENICK, author of *H3 Leadership* and *The Catalyst Leader*

"Adam is a dear friend. We often make prayer too complicated. The emphasis on honesty and brevity is great. Every follower of Jesus should read this book!"

—ROGER FREDRIKSON, pastor and author of *Learning to Dance*

"If you've ever struggled with prayer and wondered what to say, Adam Weber provides an easy-to-read, accessible guide. He takes you by the hand and leads you to the Father with gentleness and encouragement every step of the way."

—MARGARET FEINBERG, author of *Fight Back with Joy*

"I laughed. I cried. I read it out loud to my wife. In *Talking with God* Adam Weber does the seemingly impossible: he makes the topic of prayer fun, approachable, and imaginative! *Talking with God* will not just encourage your prayer life, it will kindle the fires of intimacy with God."

—DR. TIMOTHY D. WILLARD, author of *Veneer* and *Home Behind the Sun*

"Adam is currently the pastor of one of the fastest growing churches in the country, yet he is quick to share that he is a work in progress. His success as a spiritual leader is due to his humility and authenticity born of his own prayer life. What a joy to know that at any point and time we can talk with God!"

—BISHOP BRUCE R. OUGH, The United Methodist Church

"I promise, if you read this book and put the words into practice, your life will change, your work will change, your conversations will change."

—JEFF SHINABARGER, founder of Plywood People and author of *More or Less*

"*Talking with God* is not only a phenomenal book, it's an important book. In a world that is making a lot of noise, *Talking with God* presents an encouraging, challenging guide to turning that volume down and conversing with our Creator. I don't know where I'd be without Adam Weber, but I know I'd be further from Jesus. This is a MUST read."

—LUKE LEZON from @HoodJesusYo

"This is a book on prayer for the person who has heard it all or possibly nothing at all and simply wants their prayer life to grow."

—LISA WHITTLE, author of *I Want God* and *{w}hole*

"Adam delivers to us a practical guide to conversations with God. And when I say practical, I mean that I have NEVER felt like I've had a handle on a consistent prayer life. Through this book Adam has helped me take a major step toward just that. Consistency in prayer."

—CARLOS WHITTAKER, author of *Moment Maker*

TALKING
WITH
GOD

ADAM WEBER

TALKING WITH GOD

WHAT TO SAY
WHEN YOU DON'T
KNOW HOW TO PRAY

WATERBROOK

TALKING WITH GOD

Details and names in some anecdotes and stories have been changed to protect the identities of the persons involved.

Hardcover ISBN 978-1-60142-944-5
eBook ISBN 978-1-60142-945-2

Published in the United States by WaterBrook, an imprint of the Crown Publishing Group, a division of Penguin Random House LLC, New York.

WATERBROOK® and its deer colophon are registered trademarks of Penguin Random House LLC.

The Cataloging-in-Publication Data is on file with the Library of Congress.

Printed in the United States of America
2017—First Edition

10 9 8 7 6 5 4 3 2 1

SPECIAL SALES
Most WaterBrook books are available at special quantity discounts when purchased in bulk by corporations, organizations, and special-interest groups. Custom imprinting or excerpting can also be done to fit special needs. For information, please e-mail specialmarketscms@penguin randomhouse.com or call 1-800-603-7051.

Bec.
As the kids say, "We'd be in trouble without you."
Thanks for being my best friend, biggest cheerleader, and wife.
Love you so much.

Contents

ONLY THE BEGINNING

Me: How would you best describe prayer?

Roger Fredrikson:
Talking with God.

Everyone else.

A few weeks back, I received an e-mail from a friend asking if we could get together. I could tell by his words that there was something specific he wanted to talk about.

We checked our schedules and through nothing short of a miracle, we both somehow found forty-five minutes to connect over coffee the next day. We made plans to meet up at one of my favorite coffee shops in downtown Sioux Falls.[1]

I arrived a few minutes early, ordered the usual—dark coffee with one Splenda—and found a table near the front that was perfect for people-watching. Twenty minutes later, my friend arrived. He apologized for not being on time. His life is busy as he tries to be seventeen different places at once. He's getting his career off the ground. He's a dad to two young kids. And then there's his marriage. "I never thought it would all be so much work," he shared with me. He wore a smile, but you could tell his life was crazy. He was overwhelmed.

Now as a pastor, I've heard it all. Nothing really surprises me anymore. As he updated me on the status of his life, I wondered if he was struggling with something more. Had he made a mistake? Was he having an affair? I wasn't sure where our conversation was going or what he wanted to say or ask. We small-talked for ten minutes or so, and then he finally said it:

"Well, I'll just get to why I wanted to get together. I feel foolish for asking this, since I'm a grown adult. I grew up going to church, and this is something *everyone else* probably knows but me. It just looks so easy for others. But I just want to ask: How do you pray?"

He paused, took a breath, then quickly continued: "I should probably know this, right? But I don't. I feel stupid, and I wasn't sure who to ask. And again, this probably comes easy for everyone else. But again, how do you pray? Like, what do you say? Do you start with, 'Hey, God, it's me'? Is there a right or wrong way to pray? Can I screw this up?"

As my friend talked a million miles an hour, I was hoping he'd take another breath so he wouldn't pass out. I could tell he was embarrassed and felt foolish, yet he was curious and wanted to know how to pray.

I was grateful my friend was so candid and real, and honored that he trusted me enough to ask his question. But, honestly, this wasn't the first time I've been asked this question. Far from it.

———

"Everyone else" . . . they probably have prayer figured out. At least the faithful churchgoer does. And if no one else, the pastor does, right?

I can't speak for others, but I know I don't. And I'm paid to know this kind of thing.

When you open the Bible, it's clear that Jesus' followers didn't know how to pray either. In one of his first sermons, Jesus talks about and tries to explain prayer.[2]

"When you pray," Jesus said, "don't do it to be seen. Don't do it to impress others, like hypocrites often do. They might sound impressive, but they actually have it all wrong. Yup, they've missed the boat. Prayers do not need to be long, and there's no need to use big words. God isn't impressed with how we pray or the things we say. In fact, he already knows what we need, even before we start."

"Instead, when you pray, just pray like this: 'Our Father . . . '"

Again, even *followers of Jesus*—the people who hung out with Jesus himself—didn't have prayer figured out. Jesus wouldn't have talked about it with them if they had.

I'll go out on a limb and say that the majority of "everyone else" doesn't have prayer figured out either. They have questions. They feel unqualified or inadequate. They avoid prayer altogether. After all, how do you talk with the Creator of the entire universe without feeling a little intimidated?

And so, I offer this book to you. It's a book on prayer for everyone else. It's for the church outsider. The recognized sinner. The baptized and confirmed Christian. The faithful churchgoer. The follower of Jesus who feels like she falls short and the Pharisee Christian who thinks he doesn't.

This book is for those who, just like my friend, have a crazy life. It's for those who have a bunch of questions and very few answers when it comes to prayer. It's for everyone who isn't looking for a textbook explanation, a theological discussion, or even a definition of prayer. But instead is looking for a conversation about prayer they can understand and relate with. A conversation that meets them right where they are, not where they feel like they should be.

This book is for everyone else who is curious about prayer.

This book is for everyone else who wants to talk with God.

This book is for me. This book is for you.

THE GOD
WE TALK
WITH

1
Found a friend.

Tell God all that is in your heart, as one unloads one's heart,
its pleasures and its pains, to a dear friend.

—François Fénelon

Eyes closed. Hands folded. Don't move. And be as quiet as you possibly can.
At least as quiet as a five-year-old can be.

"Come, Lord Jesus, be our guest. Let this food to us be blessed. Amen."

"Now I lay me down to sleep, I pray the Lord my soul to keep. Amen."

When I was growing up, prayer was something we did only before we ate
and before we slept. Even though my mom has always been a bit of a wild
driver, we never prayed before driving anywhere. Even though bullies were
a legit concern for me at recess, we never prayed before going to school.
We never prayed randomly throughout the day. We prayed *only* before
eating and sleeping.

Is there something I should know about the food I'm eating?
What is wrong with this meatloaf?
This is meatloaf, right?
Is this my last meal?
Maybe monsters really are real and they come out once it's
* dark?*
Is someone trying to kill our family at night?
Is there a reason we pray only before we eat and sleep?

And when we prayed, we prayed the same exact words each and every time. We recited the words having no idea of what we were really saying. Repetitive. Redundant. It's just what we did.

Before bed, because my dad typically worked late, my mom would come into our room to pray with us. When we were kids, my two brothers and I shared a bedroom on the second floor of our old house.[1] The three of us were busy! *Busy* is putting it nicely. That was until we prayed. We had to be serious when we prayed. We knew we shouldn't talk or move. Or even breathe. Thankfully, our prayers were always short and sweet.

In church, however, it was a different story. And my family, the Webers, never missed church. Ever. All of us dressed in our Sunday finest. Shirts tucked in. Hair combed. Walking through the old front doors, my parents knew everyone, including the pastor. Green hymnals. Red carpet. A large wooden pulpit thing up front. An organ was off to the side. And there were wooden pews that made your rear hurt. My family sat on the right side of the room. In the same pew every week.

At good ol' American Lutheran, we prayed the exact same words each Sunday. Unfortunately, there were a lot more words than in the prayers we said at home.[2] We were supposed to keep our eyes closed, but I was a rebel and kept one eye open, scanning the room. People yawned. People mumbled. People checked the time. If Facebook had been around thirty years ago, I would have seen people checking that too. You get the point. It seemed like everyone couldn't wait for the hour to pass. I couldn't wait to talk again. I couldn't wait to run freely again. Even at five, I knew that life is short, and I couldn't wait to *live* again. Sixty minutes seemed like eternity.[3]

I sat with my short legs swinging back and forth under the pew, staring at the gray hairs on the neck of the person in front of me. To pass time, each week I counted every light on the ceiling of the sanctuary. I used to think, *If there is a God, we have to be boring him out of his mind.* I wondered if he actually listened to our prayers, because when we spoke to him, it wasn't like we expected a response. We didn't expect anything to happen. When we prayed, it seemed to be more about a box we checked. A hoop we jumped through to make some far-off being happy with us.

Who or what were we praying to? Ourselves? The thin air? I didn't know.

From an early age, I thought all of it was strange. Praying. Church. God. Baby Jesus. All of it. Weird!

My questions and doubts only continued to grow. If God was truly amazing, if he was really awesome, why were we so miserable every time we talked about him? Why didn't this supposed all-powerful God ever seem to do anything? Other than the one hour on Sunday mornings and a few quick prayers before eating and sleeping, why was he absent from our lives? Away from Sundays, it felt as if we were embarrassed to even mention God.

Even as a fourth grader, I knew that if something was awesome—a cute girl, a cool old car, next week's football game—it impacted me. I mean, with a cute girl, I couldn't talk straight around her. She was so cute and beautiful and awesome. She didn't bore me at all. Just the opposite. I couldn't stop talking about her.

By my freshman year of high school, I started to become more vocal about my questions. I also started what every Lutheran kid does: confirmation. A required two years of learning the basics of the Christian faith. At the end, you "confirm" your faith in God. It was two years of pure agony. *Lord, help!*

My clearest memory from confirmation is of having to pick a memory verse. I picked John 11:35, the shortest verse in the Bible—"Jesus wept"—but was told by my pastor I couldn't pick that one. I had to choose another. Ironically, I can't remember the other verse I chose, but I still remember John 11:35. That was the extent of what I learned in confirmation.

The day I got confirmed, my family showed up early at the church to save seats. For our small church, this was one of the biggest Sundays of the year. My friends and I wore white church robes. We each had a carnation pinned on just right. The church began filling up with family. My godparents came from North Dakota. Family came that I didn't even know I had.

During the service, my friends and I marched to the front of the church and declared our belief in God. Following the service, we had a reception at our house. After eating cake and hugging a bunch of people I barely knew, I watched as everyone left the house. It was then that I told my parents what I had been thinking the whole time. "This is the biggest lie I have ever told. And to so many people at one time." During the service, I had said that I believed in Jesus, but I clearly didn't.

We stood in our living room with the reception tables still set up. The paper plates, cups, and plastic forks still needing to be picked up. I then told my parents, "I can't wait till I get to college, when I'll be able to make decisions on my own, because God and church will never be a part of my life again."

My parents were heartbroken. Mom even cried, "Don't say that, Adam!"

They had done everything right. They faithfully brought their kids to church every Sunday, and yet I wanted nothing to do with it.

From that moment on, my parents began looking for a church that I would connect with. They set aside their own preferences and everything they knew when it came to church. We tried every church in Clark, South Dakota,[4] all six of them, and then we looked at every church outside of town. There was a tiny country church where the sermons were only eight or so minutes long. I didn't mind that one, solely because of the shorter service.

After being invited a few times to a church in another town about thirty minutes away, my parents decided to try it.[5] I thought they were nuts. Thirty minutes one way? That seemed absolutely crazy.

But I'll never forget our first Sunday there. Walking up to the church, I followed behind my parents, telling them just how stupid this was. Why in the world did we just drive thirty minutes for church? Who does this?

As we walked through the large front doors, I immediately felt like a foreigner in a strange land. We were obviously the "new people," and this church was clearly different[6] from any church I had ever been to.[7]

It was the first nontraditional worship service I had ever attended. They weren't speaking in tongues or handling snakes, but for this Lutheran, the people all seemed nuts. I felt like a kid at a zoo, seeing strange-looking animals for the first time. People were clapping, one person had his hands in the air, and they all looked happy. Maybe a little too happy.

Are they serving Kool-Aid? I wondered. *You can't smile in church. Stop smiling!*

They didn't have hymnals. My backside didn't hurt from wooden pews. And the music didn't make me want to cry tears of boredom either. Where was I?

I also noticed that they prayed differently. It was as if they were speaking *with* God, not *at* him. I had never heard people pray like that before, let alone done it myself. Ever. So strange.

Even though I thought they were all crazy, I also couldn't help but notice all the cute girls in this church.[8] They attended Watertown High School, which was much bigger than my own. Watertown was the big city to this small-town kid. I wasn't into Jesus, but the Watertown girls? That was a different story.

I wasn't counting ceiling lights in this church. Now I was counting cute girls. Knowing that going to church was an inevitable reality until I went to college, I told my parents we should come back to this church each and every week. They were thrilled that I was so interested in girls. I mean, church. Obviously.

Regardless of my reason for wanting to attend that church, God used it to slowly begin working in my life. For the first time, the pastor's words no longer flew over my head each week. Instead they began to hit me in the heart. The pastor was doing a great job selling something I didn't believe in. And over time, something began to change.

Each Sunday, it was like he was speaking right to me. As if he were reading my mind or something. How did he know so many of the things I had felt but never spoken?

I started hanging out with some of the girls and a crew of the guys, and after a while they began to invite me to their youth group on Wednesday nights. What was a young guy to do? Choose to attend only the Weber family requirement of Sunday morning church *or* possibly see more of these cute girls? Hormones won, and I gave in.

I remember thinking: *I am actually choosing to go to church? Am I feeling okay? What am I doing?*

That night I went to youth group hoping to meet a girl. Little did I know that I would end up finding a friend.

The room was packed full of kids my own age. Everyone was having a blast. They actually wanted to be there. We sang a few songs and then the youth pastor began to talk. He was right out of college and seemed normal—the first normal pastor I had ever seen. And that night, out of all things, he began to talk about prayer.

Really? Prayer? The very idea of prayer made me want to fall asleep. I had been closing my eyes and mumbling prayers my whole life; what else did I need to know about it? But what he shared about prayer that night was different from anything I had heard before.

He said, "When talking with God . . ."

Wait! *When talking with God . . . ?*

I thought this message was about prayer, about saying the same thing I had said my entire life before eating a meal or sleeping. I thought this was a talk on rambling through the same old words each Sunday while trying not to fall asleep. But he said *talking with God*?

> We can talk with God just like we do with a friend. As if he's sitting right next to us.

"When talking with God, there are different ways to pray." He continued, "Sometimes you have to sing because you're so excited and thankful for what God has done. You can't hold it in; you have to sing it.

"Sometimes when you pray, you need to get on your knees. Because you've made a mistake and you're saying you're sorry, or you're pouring out your heart to him.

"And other times," he said, "we can pray and talk with God just like we do with a friend. We can talk with God as if he's sitting right next to us."

It was the last thing I heard the youth pastor say that night.

You can talk with God? Like a friend? Really? The God who supposedly set the stars in place? The One who supposedly created me? You can talk with him? This is what prayer is?

It might seem like common sense to you, but to me it was foreign. This was different from anything I had ever heard about prayer. It was different from anything I had ever heard or known about God.

The moment I heard it, it was as if my heart leapt within me. I felt like I had found something I had unknowingly been searching for my whole life. The remainder of the night, I sat emotionless, trying to process what I was being told. *We can talk with God?*

> Not only are we able to talk with God, but he wants to talk with us.

On one occasion, Jesus was with a group of his followers and shared some things with them about who he is. He said that he is the way, the truth, and the life.[9] That he's the vine, and they are the branches.[10] And then he told them, "I don't call you servants. ... Instead, I call you friends."[11]

Now God is still God. A God so holy that angels cover their eyes when in his presence.[12] And yet he makes it clear:

Approach me. Come near to me. Talk with me. As a friend.

Crazy, huh?

It gets better. A wise Canadian once said, "*We* do not make friends with *God; God* makes friends with *us,* eh?"[13] (The "eh" was my addition.)

Hear this: not only are we able to talk with God, but we can speak with him as we do with friends. And not only are we *able* to be his friend, but he initiates that friendship with us. He initiates it with you. With me.

Again, maybe this is no big deal to you. Maybe you're totally secure with who you are as a human being that you haven't ever struggled with finding friends. But I've always struggled with wondering whether or not I fit in. Do I belong? Am I liked? Beyond that, am I loved by others? Do people want to be my friends?

Instead of having to impress people. Instead of wondering if they approve of you and enjoy hanging out with you as much as you do with them. Few things feel better than hearing someone say he wants to be your friend.

Instead of having to say it first. God initiates the friendship.

He speaks first, "I call you friend."

Not only are we able to talk with God, but he wants to talk with us.

Not only are we able to be his friend, but he wants to be ours.

That Wednesday night after youth group, halfway through the thirty-minute drive back home, I pulled my 1966 Ford Falcon Futura to the side of the road.[14] I opened my car door, got out, and just stood there as the other cars passed. Even the skeptic in me couldn't deny what I felt inside. It wasn't hormones. Something was happening within me. My heart and mind were racing with questions.

We can talk with God? Like a friend? Really?

Standing outside of my car that night, in the middle of nowhere South Dakota,[15] the stars were so bright, I felt like I could reach out and touch them. I wanted to talk with God but wasn't sure where to start. My entire life, I had never prayed a prayer that wasn't written out or memorized. With so much to say to God. With so many things bouncing around within me. The only thing I was able to say, the only thing I was able to get out:

"Lord, I just want to know if you're for real."

Looking back, it was the first time I ever truly prayed.

It was the first time I had ever really talked *with* God.

In that moment, I just wanted to know if he was who he said he was. If he existed. If he was real. I just wanted to know if I could talk with him.

My first time at youth group, I was hoping to meet a girl. Instead, I met someone who would end up becoming a friend. A guy named Jesus. I didn't know then it was a friendship that would change my life.

———

Prayer seems like it should be simple. Yet when it comes to actually praying, it often feels awkward and complicated.

I mean, what should I actually pray about?

What do I say?

Is there anything I should or shouldn't say? Do I have to speak out loud? Do I need to schedule a time with God's assistant before I can talk with him? I don't even know where to start.

To make matters worse, we've heard about prayer for so long that we feel stupid asking about it. It's like having to ask a person's name after knowing her for years. Because I really should know her name by now, I can't ask.

Then comes the craziness that is my life. And probably yours as well.

Between work, changing diapers, walking the dog, texting friends, trying to keep up with the neighbors—and the laundry—who has time to pray?

But the truth is, prayer *is* simple.

Kids are great at it. It's like talking with a good friend. It's like breathing. And what we may not know about prayer is the best part. Whether we're in the middle of a storm, living in Crazytown, or stuck in the mud, God can't wait to talk with me. With you.

Long to connect with God but don't know how? Have a job, family, schedule, kids, deadlines, a full inbox, a million things to do, yet you're curious about how to talk with God?

Do you wonder what it really looks like to pray in the midst of your life, or what to say when you don't know how to pray?

I'm asking the same questions.

Let's talk.

2

Easter Bunny.

I rose, went forth, and followed Thee.

—**Charles Wesley**

As a kid, I always thought Easter was the strangest holiday ever. Why? Each year, some random bunny would stop by our house. This bunny would supposedly come in the night and leave a bright-colored basket full of candy and fake grass for each of us. Oh, and the rabbit would hide our baskets too. As soon as my brothers and I woke up, we'd all gather in the living room and wait for my mom to announce, "All right! Go find your baskets!" We'd scramble, searching the house, looking for anything hot pink or purple. It was like the ultimate game of hide-and-seek. But even better, there was a prize at the end.

When I was a teenager, my mom—I mean, the Easter Bunny—started including a small gift in each basket as well. One year I found an Alan Jackson CD in my basket.[1] You gotta love that ol' "Chattahoochee."

I loved the Easter Bunny, but he's also kind of creepy when you think about it. According to the ever-trustworthy Wikipedia, it was the German Lutherans who started the Easter Bunny tradition. The bunny supposedly played the role of a judge, deciding if kids were good or not. If they were, they got candy. Who knows what happened if kids weren't good. Basically, next time you see the Easter Bunny, just know he's judging you and your kids. The jerk.

When I was young I loved Easter, but the older I got, the more it seemed to be just another cute holiday.[2] It was something fun for the kids. A day when we ended up eating way too many jelly beans and Cadbury eggs. A day we dressed up for church even more than on other Sundays. Once the day was done, though, Monday came and our lives went back to normal. No big deal, right?

But here's the thing: it's actually a *huge* deal.

What I didn't understand as a kid is that each Easter, we celebrated the fact that Jesus died. Like, fully dead and his body was probably smelling a bit funky. Then on the third day, just as Jesus had said would happen, he rose from the dead.

He died, but God brought him back to life.

Whether you know it or not, really, this changes everything. Especially when it comes to our ability to relate to and talk with God.

Let me explain.

———

In one of his letters, the apostle Paul wrote to a group of Christians in a city called Ephesus. He wrote about Jesus and how Jesus was raised from the dead. Paul was talking about Easter. About a risen Savior whom Paul himself once met while traveling.

Paul then reminded this group of Christians what their lives were like before they came to know Jesus. Paul wrote, "At one time you were like a dead person because of the things you did wrong and your offenses against God."[3]

Paul basically says that before Jesus enters our lives, spiritually, we're like dead people—because of the bad things we've done, our sins, and our mistakes.

I don't know about you, but as a high schooler, Paul's words seemed a bit intense to me when I first heard them from my youth pastor.

Really? Without Jesus, I'm like a dead person? Are you sure? I didn't know it was that bad.

Since the night I pulled my car to the side of the road, I had started attending youth group weekly. Each Wednesday night I made the thirty-minute drive on my own to the big city of Watertown and never missed a week. I wouldn't have admitted it then, but it became the highlight of my week. It was almost like a drug. A good drug, right?

Months earlier I had prayed and asked God to show me if he was real. In the months that followed, God made it perfectly clear that he was. I felt his presence within me. So much about life began to make sense. I was growing in my understanding of God. I began to listen to the pastor's words, no longer as a skeptic trying to pick apart what was being said but as a person curious to learn more. I couldn't wait to hear more about God.

Also, here and there I would . . . pray.

Here and there, I found myself talking with God, which, to be honest, felt awkward. So awkward. And if you're new to prayer, it will feel awkward for you too. I couldn't help myself though. I kept praying. But don't be too impressed; it was just a few words to God every once in a while. I couldn't believe I was doing it. And yet I wanted to talk with him more.

But even still, I was a dead person? I guess I didn't know that part.

It seemed a bit intense until I actually began to slow down and examine my heart, my words, my attitude, and my actions. After doing so, Paul's words began to make more sense, and I could relate with them all too well.

Spiritually, I was dead. And I didn't even know it. Until then.

————

Even today I'm often surprised and embarrassed by my own jadedness and the bitterness I too easily harbor toward others. Anger. Jealousy. Pride. The deadness is still inside of me. I often wonder, *When did I become like this? At what point did I become this person?*

Think about people and relationships in your own life. Maybe you see your deadness, your brokenness, in a former friendship where now all that remains is awkwardness and hard feelings. Maybe it's your marriage that is slowly falling apart. Maybe it's your interactions with your siblings. The relationship is dead, and it almost feels as if a part of you has died with it.

Maybe it's poor decisions that you made, and now all you're left with is regret. Or you're filled with guilt and are doing things that you can't believe you're doing. And you've maybe been doing them for so long that it no longer even bothers you. Maybe you think it's too late, you're too far gone, or you've made too many mistakes. And it's like a part of you is dead.

Where there was once excitement, life now feels mundane.

Dreams you once had are long gone.

Joy has turned to gloom.

The heart that used to be light and laid back is now hard and serious.

And it's as if a part of you is dead.

I often look at my kids and their hearts and am in awe of how new and fully alive they are. They possess complete joy.[4] They're trusting of all things and all people. They love freely and generously. They don't speak or even think negative thoughts about others. They forgive quickly and without reservation. As a parent, I wish somehow I could protect them and keep them from having to experience life. Prevent the poor decisions they will make. Protect them from the words and actions of others.

Right now they trust Jesus in every way they know how. They are fully alive.

It's a sharp contrast from my own heart and life. Seeing this clear difference reminds me often of my desperate need for God and my true state apart and away from him.

It's in these moments that I realize that I'm like a dead person without Jesus.

I'm spiritually dead without him in my life.

———

Thankfully, Paul didn't stop with telling us we're dead. He wrote on. There's more to the story.

"However, God . . . brought us to life with Christ."[5]

You were like a dead person. However, God . . . brought you back to life with Christ.

One translation says that God has "made us alive with Christ."[6]

But what does that mean? At first I was confused too.

You see, what Paul is trying to say here is this:

Without Jesus, we're like dead people.

Without Jesus, we're broken.

Without Jesus, we're filled with regret, with bitterness, with resentment.

Without Jesus, we're without hope. Without joy and peace.

Without Jesus, it's like each of us is a dead person.

However, God . . .

And this is why Easter's a big deal!

However, God . . . The same God who brought Jesus back from the dead. He makes the dead person in us come alive. He makes us new. The person we used to be is no longer. God brings you and me back to life.

And why does God do this? Listen to the rest:

"He did this because of the great love that he has for us."[7]

When we're broken, restless, and hurting. When we're dead, God brings us back to life because of his great love. The great love that he has for you. The great love that he has for me.

And if it isn't clear enough, a chapter later Paul says: "I pray that you'd have the ability to grasp how wide and how long and how high and how deep is the love of Christ and to know this love that surpasses knowledge."[8]

God's love is wide.

It's long.

It's high. So high, it reaches to the Heavens.

It's deep. Deeper than the oceans.

It's so great it can't be comprehended. It surpasses our ability to fully understand.

Mic drop, right?

Our God. His love for us is great.

Okay, so this is nice. But how is this possible? How can God bring each of us and our dead hearts back to life?

It all begins by simply speaking to God in prayer. It starts by talking with God, by inviting him to enter our lives. It begins by asking him to make us come alive. It begins by praying and speaking the words:

Jesus, I invite you into my life and everything that I am.
I'm not even fully sure what this means, but I ask you to
*   make me alive again.*
Jesus, I come and I'm broken. I'm restless. I'm empty.
My heart is angry and bitter.
I'm hurting. I'm grieving.
Lord, today it feels like a part of me, like all of me, is dead.
God, if it's possible, just as you did with Jesus, would you
*   please bring me back to life?*
I don't want to be this person anymore.
Lord, if it's possible, from the inside out, would you please
*   make me new?*
Please forgive me. Please take control of my life.
Starting today, I long to follow and have a relationship with you.

These simple words start the journey. They're not the finish line. They're only the beginning.

———

For each person, it looks different. But I spoke words like these for the first time on July 13, 1999. God had been working on me for months. I was learning more about who God is. My world was being turned upside down in the best way possible. During that time, my older brother was in college on the East Coast, and he called my mom because he was concerned that our family had joined a cult or something.

"What is up with Adam? He's talking about church!"

Even thousands of miles from home, he could tell something was happening with me.

That summer, the summer before my senior year of high school, my youth group was planning to attend a conference in Chicago, hosted at Wheaton College.[9] I couldn't sign up fast enough. Two van loads of high school kids made the trip to Chicago from South Dakota. The conference was amazing! Thousands of people singing together. Powerful messages. In that packed auditorium, I felt God's presence more powerfully than ever.

On the final day of the conference, a speaker explained how to tell people about Jesus. I have to be honest: he wasn't the best speaker. All my friends were nodding off, along with most everyone else in the room. But I listened. The speaker shared helpful words on how to invite friends to church, how to share our God-story with others, and how to share and invite a person to follow Jesus.

In that moment, I realized that I hadn't made the decision to follow Jesus myself. And I had finally come to the place where I didn't want to wait any longer. So there, in that room full of people half asleep, I silently prayed,

Jesus, I want you in my life.

In that moment, angels didn't come down from heaven and start singing. The clouds didn't part. But something did change in me.

The person I used to be was no longer. I was dead, and then I was alive.

Prior to that day, I had talked with God here and there. But I had talked with him more like an acquaintance would. Sporadically. Surface level. I spoke to him as two new classmates or coworkers would talk. But that was the day I made it clear that I wanted a relationship with God, the same relationship that God had wanted with me since before I was born. The same relationship he wants with you.

I said yes.

From that point on, prayer was no longer just talking to God here and there. I wanted more. And I now had a relationship. Which is the foundation of any deep, meaningful conversation, right?

That day, I started a relationship with Jesus, which is the very foundation of prayer. I couldn't wait to find out more about God, and I was excited to talk with him more.

The truth is that most people pray, Christians and non-Christians alike. People who go to church and those who don't. Everybody prays, sometimes without knowing it. When we're on a plane, as it takes off. For some reason we pray. When we're wheeled into an operating room, even if it's a simple surgery, we pray. When our favorite sports team is in a close game, we bite our nails and we pray. It just happens. We might not even hear the words we're saying, words whispered under our breath:

Lord, help my team to win!

God, help me pass this test.

Lord, help my mom be okay.

God, I hope this pilot knows how to fly.

Jesus, why am I doing this?

Whether we're pursuing God or not, the words, our prayers, just come out.

However, something changes when we have a relationship with God. Because our hearts are alive, we're alive. And because we're alive, our prayers come alive. Instead of just speaking words *to* someone, we're talking *with* someone. With God.

There's a foundation. A relationship. With Jesus.

———

One night shortly after praying at that conference, I was with a friend. We were driving,[10] and out of nowhere he said to me, "Adam, something just seems so different about you. Can I ask what it is?"

At the time, my friend was at a place similar to where I'd been just a few months earlier, before becoming a Christian myself. He thought God, church, and everything connected with it was foolish, all garbage.

That night was one of the first times I realized what God had done and was doing within me. Something had changed, and even my friend noticed. I was shocked by his words, that even he could see that something had happened to me. I wasn't the same person anymore, he said.

I was alive.

Yes, I still had faults. I still made mistakes. I was far from perfect. But I was no longer the same.

That night, all I could tell my friend was that Jesus had changed me. As I rambled, I told him I couldn't explain it. That it didn't all add up. That I still had doubts. And yet Jesus had given me a fresh start, a completely new beginning. I told him that I had prayed and asked God to come into my life. Even though I was new to it myself, I tried to explain to my friend that we could talk with God.

———

Unlike the Easter Bunny, who tries to decide if we're good or not, if we deserve a reward or not, if we deserve anything, God sends us Jesus. God gives us the gift of relationship with him through Jesus, despite our mistakes. We don't deserve the relationship. On our own, we're not good enough to have that relationship. Yet that's exactly why Jesus came, to make a relationship with God possible. And even if you were the only person on earth, Jesus would still have died on the cross for you and you alone. He loves you regardless. Unconditionally.

You were like a dead person.

However, God—the same God who brought Jesus back from the dead—makes you and me come alive. Because of the great love that he has for us.

God can't wait to have a relationship with us, a relationship that will bring us back to life.

Prayer is the starting point for that relationship.

3

Party of the year!

I am the prodigal son every time I search for unconditional love where it cannot be found.

—Henri Nouwen

If you had asked me when I was growing up to describe Christians, I would have used words like *boring, miserable,* and *lame*—on a good day.

It seemed that everyone I knew who actually talked about Jesus was either a super serious, uptight person or flat-out weird. All I could think was, *I don't want to be like you.*

And when it came to God himself, I knew of him only from a distance. Although my family had a lot of Bibles, we never actually read them. They stayed stacked up in the bottom corner of one of our closets. I grew up in the church and rarely missed, but I knew very little about God. And I just assumed that God and Jesus and whoever else was in the Bible were the same as the Christians I knew. Uptight or weird. Maybe both. Sadly, I don't think my upbringing was an isolated experience. I've met far too many friends with similar stories.

Even after a few months of talking sporadically with God, and even after starting my new friendship with him, I had a lot of questions. *When we pray, who is the God we're speaking with? What's he like?* I didn't fully know, but I wanted to find out.

Based on my experience of church, I had always assumed that Jesus never laughed and that he probably wasn't fun to be around. I also assumed he was a bit of a party pooper. So I figured I probably needed to be cautious with my words to him. Cautious with my prayers so I didn't say the wrong thing to him. I didn't want to upset him or anything.

Yet when I actually began to read through the Bible, I discovered the complete opposite to be true. Truth is, Jesus loved to have a good time.

He enjoyed celebrations and he enjoyed parties. Who would have thought?

One of my all-time favorite stories in the Bible is found in the book of Luke.[1] We're told at the start of the story that Jesus was with a bunch of "tax collectors and sinners," the outsiders of his day.[2] These were people who had made big mistakes, and everyone knew it. These were the people you didn't want to associate with (or be associated with). Basically, if you were a good religious person, you *wouldn't* be hanging out with them. And yet here was Jesus, sitting with them. He even ate with them. The super religious people couldn't believe what they were seeing and they began mumbling about Jesus, "Why is he doing this? What is he thinking?"

In response to their grumbling, Jesus shared a few stories to better explain what the heart of God is like. He told one story about a lost sheep and another about a lost coin. Then he told a story about a man who had two sons. This story is known as the story of the prodigal son. And it's a story of forgiveness and grace. But it's also a passage that gives great insight into prayer. It shows us much about the God we're able to talk with.

As the story goes, the younger of the two sons came to his father and asked for his inheritance. In Jesus' day this would have been completely unheard of. You see, you only got your money after your dad died. So the son was saying, "Dad, I'd rather have the money than have you alive."

In this day, most dads would have had this son beaten and sent away for making a request like this. The dad would have been embarrassed and completely heartbroken. And the neighbors and the whole town would have been talking about that spoiled, deadbeat, worthless pile of a son. But instead of beating his son, the father in Jesus' story fulfilled the boy's request. He divided up his estate and gave half of it to his younger son. And when the kid got his share, we're told that he quickly gathered up his things and traveled to a land far away. It was as if he packed up and headed to Winnipeg. Maybe to hang out with Celine Dion and Justin Bieber?

————

I've read through this story countless times, yet it still gets to me. Why did the son leave home? Why would he ever decide to do this to his dad? We're not given a specific reason, but it seems like he was simply looking for the freedom to do whatever he wanted. He wanted to go looking for a better life. One he thought he would find on his own, away from his dad.

Dad, can I just have my money now? Because I'd rather do my own thing.

Dad, this has been good, and thank you for covering my needs, but I think I'm going to go my own way. Because this is my life.

Dad, I want to respect you, but I want to call my own shots and don't want to be tied down. I don't want to say I know better than you, but I kind of do. And I'm looking for a different and better life than the one I have with you.

Think about our own relationship with God. Doesn't this seem to be the story of our lives? I know it sounds eerily familiar to me. For me, my words have often sounded something like this:

God, you're great and all, but I'm doing well without you. And this is my life. I just want to enjoy it!

I'm glad you want me to know you, but I don't like feeling so restricted.

I know that my priorities should probably be different than they are, but I'm going to go do my own thing. I'm an adult. Don't worry. I'll be fine.

I feel like I'm making pretty good decisions on my own.

I'll still do the church thing on Sundays when I can.

And I'll pray when I think about it.

You're welcome to be a part of my life, but this is my life, so I hope you can respect it.

Can anyone else relate?

———

Jesus' story continues. The son asked for his money, packed up his things, and headed for a land far away.[3] Once there, we're told, he quickly burned through his money, living it up. One Bible translation says that he "wasted all his money in wild living."[4]

At the same time he ran out of money, a famine hit the area. So he went from wild living to living out in the fields with pigs. Eating worse than the pigs.

It's crazy. The son had gone looking for a better life. He was confident, so sure that he'd find it on his own. And yet he quickly ended up finding the complete opposite.

Instead of enjoying his freedom, he was now just trying to survive. Instead of finding a better life, he found the worst life imaginable.

We're told that the son finally "came to his senses."[5] He realized that it would be better to go back home. His life would be better working for his dad, even as a slave, than it would be staying where he was, living on his own.

So he decided to go back home and confess his wrongs to his dad (who represents God). And on his way home, the son actually began practicing what he would say to his dad.

Have you ever done this with God? Ever tried to figure out the exact words to pray? Ever agonized over what to say and what not to say? Wondered if God would be angry with you, or at least a little upset? Because he's probably super serious, right? Maybe you've ignored and distanced yourself from God for years because of it, and you think, *After making so many mistakes, he probably doesn't want me to talk with him at all.*

Yet Jesus tells us that while the son was still far off, his father saw him and was filled with compassion. His dad ran, embraced him, and kissed him.

Not the response he expected, the son began to confess, declaring, "Father, I have sinned against heaven and against you."[6] Translation: "I'm so sorry, Dad!"

The son asked to be made his dad's slave. Yet what did the dad do?

He immediately told his servants to . . .

Bring out the best robe they had and put it on his son. Put a ring on his finger and sandals on his feet. Fetch the prized livestock and slaughter it for a feast. Something that took hours to prepare. Something that was done only for esteemed guests.

And then the dad proclaimed, "We must celebrate!"

Why?

"Because this son of mine was dead and has come back to life!

"He was lost and is found!"[7]

And so they began to party!

We're then told that while this was taking place, the other brother was out in the field working, and that as he was coming in, getting closer to home, he heard "music and dancing."[8]

Get this. The music was so loud that it could be heard in the fields.[9] It's believed the music was from flutes and bagpipes. I love that. And for the record, I picture them in Scottish kilts!

"Bring a robe, ring, and sandals. Throw a lamb on a grill. Start the music and don't forget about the bagpipes!"

Once again, here's the story: The son committed an outrageous crime against his dad. He told his dad he was better off without him and left home. Yet when the son returned, the father threw a party. And not just a party, but the party of all parties!

In case you forgot, the reason Jesus told this story in the first place is that the uptight religious people were giving him a hard time for sitting and talking with sinners and tax collectors. Jesus told this story to better explain who God is. That the heart of God is like a dad who throws a party![10]

———

When we pray, who is the God we're speaking with? What is he like?

We're not talking to a rule-obsessed, boring, uptight God. Growing up, I based my understanding of God solely on Christians who were much like the Pharisees in this story. Unfortunately, there are followers of Jesus who aren't much like him, including myself from time to time. Sadly, we Christians seem to grumble and mumble a lot. Often we are uptight and just plain weird.

While that might be true of some followers of Jesus and religious people in general, it's not true of God. He's just the opposite. He's full of life. There's joy in his presence. He's quick to celebrate. And God has a great sense of humor!

When we pray, we're talking with a Father who gives his deadbeat kid a ring, the best robe, and bagpipes when he comes home.

This is the God we're in a relationship with. This is the God we're coming near to. This is the God that we're talking with.

When we talk with God, we're talking with a God who loves to throw parties.

Knowing this changes prayer. At least it does for me. I don't need to be uptight and serious when I pray. Yes, it's good to have a healthy reverence of and respect for God. But you don't have to be emotionless or somber. There's no need to practice our prayers before speaking them. God is abundantly loving and gracious. It isn't a sin to smile or laugh when we're speaking with God. For God's sake, we should express joy and laughter and have fun. These emotions come from God. He's the one who created us with the ability to laugh.

I can talk with God about something rad that happened in my day. I can laugh with him about something hilarious that took place. Even more so, I speak with him when I've screwed up. When I've blown it in life.

Whenever I decide to come home. Whenever you decide to come home. This is the God we come home to: a party-throwing God. Have I mentioned he's wild about us?

The more time I spend with God, the more time I spend reading the Bible and talking with him, the more I see his heart and who he truly is. When we pray, a party-throwing God is the God we're talking with.

Just to be clear, it's deeper though. It's one thing to throw a party when a person deserves it or has a special occasion. And it's another thing to throw a party when you'd be justified in throwing rocks or insults at someone. The truly good news about God is this: No matter how far we are away from home, no matter how long we've been away from God's side—days, months, years, a lifetime, even if we've walked away from him, if we've been out look-ing for life on our own, if we haven't talked with God in years, or ever—we can still come home any time. We can still speak with him.

At any point, we can say the words:

Father, I'm ready to come home.
Lord, I've been searching my whole life for a better life apart
*   from you.*
As a result, I'm tired, and I'm broken.
I'm lost, and I want to be found.
I don't want to be away from you any longer.

I want to be with you. I want to talk with you.
Jesus, I'm ready to come to your party!

And when we do say those words, he doesn't say, "I told you so." Instead of beating us over the head with our failures, instead of making us a slave, instead of making us look like a fool, he throws a party.

Why?

Because his sons and daughters were dead, and we've come back to life.

We were lost and now are found.

———

A couple of years ago, I got a glimpse of the heart that God has for us, particularly when we're far from him, not talking with him. I got a look at how God feels when we're lost.

My wife's folks came to town, and we visited them at their hotel.[11] All our nephews and nieces were there as well, so kids were everywhere. My in-laws got a suite at the hotel, which consisted of three large rooms. (This makes it sound much cooler than it was.)

At one point, the entire family was on the first floor of the hotel and we all decided to head back to the suite on the second floor. But the kids ran ahead. We told them to stop. We told them to stay close to us, but they didn't listen. They didn't want to wait for us slow-pokey parents, so they ran up the stairs together. The adults followed behind.

When we all got to the room, the kids were playing and having fun. But after about fifteen, or maybe even twenty, minutes someone randomly asked: "Where's Grayson?"

Grayson is my daughter, who was four years old at the time. And, come to think of it, I hadn't seen her either.

At first it seemed like no big deal because she had to be somewhere in the room. So we checked the first room and the first bathroom; I knocked and she wasn't in there. We went to the next room, and checked the bathroom. She wasn't there. We then looked through the last room and she wasn't there either. In a matter of seconds, it had become crystal clear that my daughter was nowhere in the suite, and she hadn't been with us for more than fifteen minutes!

Complete panic. Absolute fear! Honestly, I can't remember a time I've ever felt like that.

I didn't say a word. I couldn't speak. I just ran. I ran out of the room, as fast as I possibly could. I first ran to the elevator, and when it didn't immediately open, I ran to the stairs. All I could think was that I needed to get to the parking lot to make sure Grayson wasn't with someone else. *I need to find her!*

I sprinted down the stairs.

My whole family—aunts and uncles, cousins, everyone—searched frantically. It was the first time I'd ever seen my father-in-law run.

Out of breath, I finally made it to the first floor, and there I spotted the hotel manager. She was holding my Grayson in her arms. The lady didn't have to ask. She could just tell by the look on my face that I was the dad.

I ran to Grayson and grabbed her. I held her in my arms, hugging her. Probably a little too tightly. I asked her, "Baby, what happened?"

My little girl was crying uncontrollably, and she said, "Daddy, I was lost. And I was scared."

We found out later what had happened. When the kids ran off to the suite without the parents, Grayson did the same, but she was slower than the other kids. Because she couldn't keep up, she lost sight of the others and ended up on the third floor instead of the second. She got lost.[12]

As I held and hugged her the whole way back to the room, my heart still racing, what did I say to Grayson?

I didn't mention that she should have listened and stayed close to me.

I didn't mention that she shouldn't have run ahead.

I didn't mention that it was her fault and not mine.

Instead I just kept telling her, over and over again, how much I love her.

"Baby, Daddy loves you so much. I love you so much! I'm so glad I found you!"

We talked all the way back to the room, our faces literally inches apart. I couldn't take my eyes off her, and her eyes didn't leave me. I wasn't grumbling or mumbling. I wasn't hoping that she'd learned her lesson. Every part of me was rejoicing. Audibly, I was thanking God. I was so glad I could speak with her, and she with me. My words were a combination of crying and laughing. Craughing?

When we got to the room, joy filled the place once again. Everyone hugged her, and we couldn't stop. It was a celebration in the deepest sense.

Then I went into a room by myself and had a good cry. I cried long enough that my ribs hurt from doing so. As I lay there trying to calm down, I couldn't help but think about God's heart toward us. It's the same heart I have for my little girl, but infinitely greater.

And I couldn't help but think about God's love for you and for me. And about how his heart breaks whenever we're far away, how it *aches* when we're not by his side.

Our party-throwing God is crazy about you, and he longs to be with you.

He wants to speak with you face to face.

He longs to talk with you.

When we pray, this is the God we're talking with.

THE WAY
WE PRAY

4

Short. Simple. Honest.

The fewer the words, the better the prayer.

—**Martin Luther**

Help my butt to feel better.

Thank you for mac-n-cheese.

Help me to not dream about monsters.

Thank you that next month is my birthday.

Help my sister to not be so mean anymore.

I'm not sure why I can't see you.

Help me to find a friend at recess tomorrow.[1]

I'm never quite sure what my kids are going to say, let alone pray.

In the Weber household, we have four kids. Yes, four. All under the age of ten.[2] We also have a minivan. Because we're cool like that. When did this become my life? I'm not sure. But each night after my four yahoos have their pj's on and their teeth brushed, we pray.

Don't picture four kids beautifully kneeling in a row at the end of their beds. Picture them playing with Legos, hanging upside down, constantly interrupting, and annoying each other. It's the opposite of eyes closed and mumbling. When we pray, it's complete chaos. (Yes, I'm a pastor, and no, you can't judge my family.) I start praying, and they randomly add things throughout the prayer.

They pray for their stuffed animals. They pray for the Tooth Fairy to come. They pray for their grandpa to feel better. They pray for the owies on their knees to go away. Again, I'm never quite sure what they're going to pray for, but I know it'll be short, simple, and honest.

They just say it. I mean, pray it. There's no fluff, it's not long and drawn out, and they don't beat around the bush. They don't talk using a different voice or different words than they use elsewhere. They say what they feel, and they feel what they say. Short. Simple. Honest.

––––––

It's short.

Often it's only one sentence long. Sometimes just a few words.

Jesus, thank you for the sun today.

In the middle of winter in South Dakota, the sun is a big deal. So they thank God for it.

Thank you that next month is my birthday.

A month is like a decade to a four-year-old. Yet birthdays are awesome. So they give God a shout-out.

They've never prayed a four-point sermon. For them, there's no certain length that makes a good prayer. They say what they want to. They say what's needed. Hardly anyone likes a long-winded prayer. Neither do they. I don't want to speak for God, but I'm guessing he might feel the same way. Kids keep it short.

———

It's simple.

My kids don't pray in the King James Version. There are no thous or shalts. When praying, they sound the exact same way they do when speaking with anyone else. They don't use big, fancy words. You don't need a dictionary to understand what they are saying. They're not praying to be heard by others. They're not praying to impress God but to talk with him.

Jesus, help me to find someone to play with at recess.
God, I'm not sure why I can't see you.

———

It's honest.

Kids keep it real yo. They speak from the heart. They pray what they mean, not what they should. When they're happy, they tell God. When they're sad, they let him know. When they're scared, they tell him why. When they want something, they ask him for it. When their butts hurt because they're still learning how to properly wipe?

God, help my butt to feel better.

What they feel is what they say. There's no filter. It's honest.

———

But they're just kids, right?

They're so cute. They're so innocent. They're so uneducated when it comes to God. They don't even know. In a few years, when they get older, when they know more, they'll learn how to pray the "right way." For the "right things." Until then, their wrong prayers are just sweet and innocent.

Right?

Wrong.

> Pray like a kid? Yup, become like a child.

At one point in the Bible, the twelve disciples were chatting about which of them was the greatest. About who was the best among them. When they couldn't agree, they approached Jesus and asked him their question. "Who is the greatest in the kingdom of heaven?"[3] Essentially they're asking, "Hey Jesus, who among us is the most important? Which one of us is the best?"

Jesus' response? He didn't ask one of the experienced fishermen to stand up. He didn't tell an educated doctor to step forward. He didn't look to a wise priest for his thoughts. Instead, he called out to a young kid and asked him to come over to sit by him. And what did Jesus say? He said, "Become like this little child."[4] What? Like a little kid? Have faith like a little kid? Even pray like a kid? Yup, become like a little kid. Pray like a child. The disciples must have been shocked.

What do we have to learn about prayer from kids?

Everything.

———

Keep it short.

Just to be clear, there's nothing wrong with long prayers. The point is that they're not required to be long. They're not better because they're long. We shouldn't randomly add things just so our prayers are a certain length.

You don't need to pad your prayers like you did your eighth-grade book report, rambling at the end to reach a certain length. God just wants to hear from you.

Sometimes using only a few words is better. When standing in awe of a star-filled night, a person doesn't stand there talking. Instead he sums things up with a simple "Wow!" That says it all. Instead of speaking, you just take it all in.

Sometimes I have long conversations with my friends, but typically they're short. Most days they last a couple of minutes. Maybe just a text. That doesn't mean our interactions are shallow. With close friends we're able to speak from the heart using a few words.

Thinking about you today and the meeting you're in.
Thankful for you. It's a gift to have someone like you to
  talk with.

My wife and I don't even have to speak to communicate. We're able to say so much just by looking at each other. We know what the other is thinking without a word. I can walk in the door after a rough day at work, and she just knows.[5]

When talking with God, the same is true.

God, thank you for this beautiful morning. You're an
awesome Creator.

Jesus, fill me with your patience and joy. I'm grateful
you're with me.

Lord, give me the words to speak to my friend who's
hurting.

> Don't try to sound all prim and proper. Don't use strange religious words. Just talk with God.

Whether our words are few or many, our God loves hearing from us throughout the day. He loves hearing about and being a part of our day. Like a parent, he'd much rather hear a quick "hello" from us than nothing at all. To this day, every time I call my parents, whether we talk for three minutes or half an hour, they often put me on speakerphone so they both can hear me. We talk about my kids. We talk about their day and mine. And at some point in every conversation, even though I'm now thirty-five years old, they say, "We always love when you call, Adam. We're so glad that you did. We love talking with you."

––––––––

Keep it simple.

It's crazy how we can make something so simple into something so complex. As human beings, we like to make things more difficult than they need to be.

We also feel the constant urge to impress others by looking and sounding better than we really are. Have you ever seen this in a friend or coworker? Depending on whom she is with, she talks and acts like a completely different person. It's annoying. It makes you think less of the person. Yet we do the same thing with God himself.

Do you ever wonder how many times God has thought:

> *Who is this person? Adam, is that you? Where is the
>   Adam I know?*
> *Who is this guy who sounds like he's reading out of a
>   thesaurus?*

We don't need to impress God. He's the one who wants to be friends with us. Just be you. The *real* you, not some weird version of you. Don't try to sound all prim and proper. Don't use strange religious words. Don't worry about saying the wrong thing. Don't make it complicated. Just talk with him. We can't mess it up! My best advice on prayer: say exactly what's inside you.

Don't edit your words. Say whatever you're feeling. Tell God in a few words. But don't hesitate to ramble either. Just let it come out.

Jesus, I love you. That's all. I just wanted to say I love you.

Lord, I feel stupid. I made a mistake. Forgive me.

Father, I'm not sure what decision I'm supposed to make. Help me.

Jesus isn't looking for a show. He's not looking to be amazed by our words or impressed by our knowledge or our extravagant prayers. Jesus specifically said the opposite about prayer.[6] More than anything, he wants just to talk with us. Keep it simple.

———

Keep it honest.

Who knows how many times I've prayed what I thought I should pray or what I thought God wanted to hear rather than what I was actually feeling and wanting to say. I tell God that I'm thankful when I'm really upset. Or that I'm grateful for his peace when I don't feel any.

That's called lying!

One of my favorite psalms is also one that's a bit scary if you stop and think about it. In it, David talks about how God sees everything and is everywhere.

He sees us when we wake up. He sees us when we're traveling and going from here to there. And then David says this:

> Before a word is on my tongue
>   *you* know it completely, O LORD.[7]

Isn't that a beautiful and terrifying thing to know about God? He knows *everything* I'm thinking and *everything* I'm going to say without me even saying it? Being fully exposed before God is scary, isn't it?

In knowing this, though, I have to think, *If God sees it all within me, why would I keep it in? I mean, why wouldn't I be honest and say what's really on my mind?*

David knew this truth well. Reading the psalms, at times it seems as if David's lost his mind. He's happy one second, mad the next. He asks God to save him and kill others. He questions God constantly. David doesn't hold anything back. He's raw. I think that's why people love the psalms so much.

Just as he did in David, God sees everything in us. He sees all the unspoken words within us. So, be honest and say them.

God, I'm mad that you haven't healed my dad!

Lord, I'm tired and I feel like I'm in over my head at work.

Jesus, I'm restless. I'm struggling with anxiety. I need your peace.

Father, when am I ever going to catch a break in life?

As a dad, I'm disappointed when my kids make a mistake or hurt me. But nothing hurts worse than when they lie to me. I want to hear what my kids are feeling and going through. I want them to be honest, even if the truth is hard to hear. I also want to know their needs and even their wants, the desires of their heart.

Thinking about my own prayers, I realize that I often don't talk with God about something because it feels selfish. Ever feel that way? I feel bad asking him for things. I feel like I should probably pray only for others. There are so many needs in this world, why should I bother God with my small problems and wants? Truth is, our Father loves to hear our requests. Nothing is too big or too small to share with him, and he wants to provide generously for our needs.

———

After the kids and I finish praying each night, we say amen and exchange I love yous, and I hug each of them. Then, after I close their bedroom doors, they fall asleep almost immediately. Without a care in the world. All the cares they did have were just handed over to God.

A couple hours later, after watching an episode of *The Goldbergs* and the nightly news, Bec and I get ready for bed ourselves. (Don't picture my tighty-whities.) We climb into our bed, and before we go to sleep, we pray together. Unlike the kids though, I often lie awake thinking. Tossing and turning and stressing about the exact things we just prayed for and so many other things that were left unsaid. My heart and ability to trust God is so much different than my kids'. I'm actually jealous.

Lord, help me to become like a little kid.
*Help me to approach you. To talk with you. To trust you
like a child.*

When it comes to talking with God, what can we learn from kids?

Pretty much everything. Keep it short, simple, and honest.

5

Crazytown.

The more you pray, the easier it becomes. The easier it
becomes, the more you'll pray.

—Mother Teresa

I honestly don't remember when I moved to Crazytown.[1] I know it's been
years. But I do remember first visiting back in college.[2]

Back then, Crazytown consisted of writing papers, eating cheap pizza,
working, trying to impress girls, doing homework, playing Super Mario Kart,
sleeping, and every so often, going to class. Four years of pure happiness.

But even at the time, life felt crazy. Each day I wanted to do more than I had
time for, more than what could fit into a single day. Little did I know that my
visits to Crazytown were just beginning. I didn't even have a clue. No idea!

After college, I got married. This meant having to think about someone
other than myself. Laundry. Dishes. Taking out the trash. Pretending to enjoy

shopping together. Trying to be somewhat clean and considerate so I could stay married.

Then graduate school.[3] I wrote longer papers. Did odd jobs to pay for school. Went to class. And, I know, I probably should have exercised more.

Then, somehow, our first baby showed up. As it turns out, babies aren't delivered by storks. Actually I'm still unsure where they come from, but we were now fully responsible for another living, breathing human being, and there was no instruction manual included. The band R.E.M. said it perfectly. "It's the end of the world as we know it."[4]

Diapers. Poop. Spit-up. Pee. No sleep. Trying to be a dad. *Lord, help!*

Then a real job. Like, a real one. More responsibility. Deadlines.

Facebook was created. Then Twitter. Then Instagram. Then Snapchat.[5] Embarrassing amounts of time wasted. If I ever did have any extra time, it's now completely gone. Can I get an "Amen"?

Then we bought a house, and, without even knowing it, I had officially *moved* to Crazytown. The house—it had a lawn that needed to be mowed. Things broke. Sidewalks had to be shoveled. Lightbulbs needed changing. And for some reason, we felt obligated to paint every room in the house a different color every couple of years. Is it too late to move back into a college dorm?

Three more kids showed up. I still can't believe I have four. And we needed a dog, right?[6] Why not get a chicken too? Heck, let's make it four chickens.[7]

Crazytown. It's where I lived then, and where I still live today. It's all that I know. Honestly, after living here for so long, I can't imagine living anywhere else.

Sound familiar? Oh, you live here too? I thought I saw you around.

Your version of Crazytown may look completely different from mine, which looks completely different from the next person's. But in general, if you're anything like me, most days you're just trying to keep your head above water. Trying to keep all the plates spinning at once. All ducks in a row. If you're anything like me, you're just trying to survive another day.

Between work, deadlines, kids, schedules, diapers, homework, social media, and whatever life throws your way, who has time for anything else? And be honest, more money would be nice, but more than anything, you just wish you had more time, right?

And in the midst of juggling sixteen different things at once, who has time for God? More specifically, in the midst of Crazytown, who has time to pray?

Is there a required amount of time in a day someone has to pray? Like a bare minimum to shoot for? I hate to even ask, but what's the requirement for a pastor?

———

The apostle Paul wrote a really helpful letter to a group of Christians in a city called Thessalonica. *Where was that?* I can't pronounce it either.

Near the end of Paul's letter though, he told people what their lives, our lives, should look like as followers of Jesus. Here are a few of the random things he mentioned.[8]

"Encourage each other."

All right. I'll try.

"Do good to one another."

Okay, that's not too bad.

"Rejoice always."

I guess I can try to be thankful or something? I can probably do that.

"Pray without ceasing."

Come again?

Without ceasing. Continually. Always. It can also be translated as "Never stop."

Oh, okay. Wonderful. This pretty much seems . . . impossible.

Have I mentioned where I live?

This isn't realistic! I don't have nearly the time. I have too much going on. I can't commit to doing anything more than I'm already doing. I'm trying to get better at saying no to things. And if I do miraculously have spare time, I just want to unplug and collapse on my couch. And catch up on important things, like *SportsCenter.*

I mean, I can maybe throw a prayer up to God here and there. When I have time. Maybe on Sundays at church or during the Bengals football game that afternoon. Or when I really *need* to pray. At most, I'll say a quick prayer as I roll out of bed each day. Sound good? But pray without ceasing? I can't seem to concentrate on anything for even five minutes without checking Twitter. (Just being up front.) Sorry, Paul, I'm not even going to attempt this because I know I'll fail. Prayer is great, but this simply isn't going to work.

Even if I truly wanted to pray nonstop, I just can't right now. Hopefully, once I finish school, okay? In a couple of years when the kids are older? In one month, this project at work should be complete, and once things settle down a bit more, I'll give prayer more of an effort. But I just can't take on anything else right now. And, really, how is this possible for *anyone*?

———

Back in the 1600s, there was a guy named Brother Lawrence. Picture a dude wearing a brown robe, living in a monastery, probably chanting prayers or something. He's recognized by most as the expert on this "pray without ceasing" thing, and he explained it quite well.[9]

Rather than thinking of prayer as something separate and set apart from the rest our day, just one more thing we need to cram into the week or add on top of life, Brother Lawrence explained that prayer was meant to be done *in the midst of it.*

In the midst of our day. In the midst of our week. In the midst of our life. Even in Crazytown. We can pray.

Are you washing dishes? Brother Lawrence would tell us to acknowledge and talk with God while washing dishes.

Are you running errands? Talk with God while running errands.

Is your day slammed with meetings?

Are you running from one thing to the next?

Are you painting yet another room in your house?

Cleaning up poop from your kid, your dog, or both at the same time?

Feel like you're the actual mayor of Crazytown?

Pray without ceasing. Continually. Always. Never stop.

Talk with God in the *midst* of it all.

Okay, so that's nice in theory, but is it really possible?

For me, this sure seemed impossible when I first heard it. But as a brand-new Christian, I began to get serious about my relationship with God during the first semester of my freshman year of college. Until that point, I loved the Lord but still lived two different lives. I was one Adam with one group of friends and a different version of myself with the next group. In high school,

I had two completely different groups of friends. With one group, I never talked about God, and with the other, talking about God was the reason we gathered.

When I wasn't with my church friends, no one would have associated God with me. No one would have mentioned God and my name in the same sentence. By the time I got to college, I was tired of trying to live two different lives based on who I was with. I needed and wanted God in every part of my life. Every part of my day. I was ready to make a change.

Several weeks into my freshman year, I felt God challenging me: *Adam, are you willing to follow me with your whole heart? With all that you are?*

One night in my dorm room, I decided I was.[10] I wanted to fully follow him. All in. I knew talking with God more often would be a huge part of that. I began intentionally speaking with God more throughout my day. In the morning. Before meals. While walking to my next class. Before going to sleep. If something reminded me of God, I took the time to acknowledge him. To sit with him. To talk with him. Often, I wrote a short prayer on a notecard and carried it in my pocket, or I'd keep it on my nightstand, reminding myself to pray. I needed that constant reminder.

What started as a very disciplined and intentional effort, prayer slowly began to show up more and more often throughout my day on its own. And I stress *slowly*. It took time.

Also, I'll be honest, even as a pastor, there are days—embarrassingly, sometimes weeks—when I don't say a word to God. I let the craziness, busyness, and hurriedness of my days take over. And by the end of those days, I can tell that I've lived without God being a part of them. And I feel distant from

God. I can't sense his presence. His joy, peace, and goodness begin to vanish from within me.

Truth be told, we will always be able to find reasons why we don't have the time (or energy) to pray. Whether you're a college student, stay-at-home mom, second-grade teacher, pastor, or busy grandma, each of us can come up with an argument for why your life is out of control. So finding time to pray isn't easier for some than for others. That's a cop-out answer. Instead of making excuses, we have to get to the place where we so clearly realize our desperate need for talking with God that it becomes a priority. Like we *have* to pray. Life is so busy that we *need* to talk with God every day. Even when life is nuts, we find time for the things we value. Prayer can be one of those things.

Instead of it being another daily chore, something changes when prayer slowly becomes as natural as breathing. When we figure out that it no longer takes energy. Instead, prayer fills us with it. Prayer fills us with life. It gives us the ability to love our coworker and not strangle him. It allows us to be patient instead of frustrated with our kids, or someone else's. Prayer makes it possible to have a positive attitude on the crappiest of days. I'm beginning to realize that unless I am in constant conversation with God, I have little love, little patience, little gratitude, and a terrible attitude on my own.

Earlier this summer, I came home from work one day to find that one of the neighbor kids had climbed on our backyard fence and broken a board.

Now, that really isn't a big deal, right? But for some reason, it was a big deal for me that day. (Don't judge!) I was tired from a long day at work and just wanted to relax. When I got home, the last thing I wanted was yet another item on my to-do list, and I was grumpy about it. Let's just say that I was not walking or talking with Jesus. All I could think was, *Darn neighbor kids! Stinking kids! And where are their parents?*

I grabbed a couple of screws and got my drill, because I'm handy like that. Okay, so maybe I'm not handy at all. But I headed to the backyard to fix the fence, mumbling as I walked. My oldest son, Hudson, seeing I was flustered said, "Dad, they didn't do it on purpose. They were just talking with us and it broke."

All I could think back was, *Does it look like I care? Stinking kids. Breaking my fence! I have a right to be angry about something like this!*

As I was fixing the fence, I continued to mumble, when suddenly out of nowhere it was like God was right there. And it was as if he was saying, *Really? What? Who are you to complain about these things? Don't you know I gave you that fence? And everything in your house, for that matter? You are the last person who should be sounding like a jerk!*

Whoa. I almost physically fell to my knees.

In that moment, I saw how ugly my attitude was and automatically I started praying, asking that God would fill me with his love and patience. I prayed that my attitude would become more like his. I needed to talk with God, and as soon as I did, my heart softened. My tightened body relaxed. My attitude changed as I stood there working on the fence.

I spoke words to Hudson that he already knew. "I'm sorry, buddy. I was wrong for being upset. The kids didn't break the fence on purpose. One broken board isn't worth acting like I did. Sorry."

———

When prayer becomes second nature like breathing, we gain the ability to make it through each day and whatever craziness comes our way. There's no need to "fit prayer into our day" because we can't imagine a day without it. We no longer have to think about praying; we just do it.

Pray without ceasing.

It centers us.

Keeps us sane.

Gives us strength.

Carries us through.

Rearranges our priorities.

Fills us with joy.

Covers us with peace.

Allows us to extend grace.

Even better?

It connects us with the One who treads water for us when we're unable to swim ourselves. The Ultimate Plate Spinner who helps us discern which plates are actually worth spinning.

It opens communication with the One who created us and knows us better than we know ourselves, the One who knows the ins and outs of life.

It's crazy. We tend to separate prayer from the place where we need it the most—in the midst of our Crazytown lives.

Here's the truth, though: something changes when prayer is no longer just one more thing in our day but becomes the most important thing.

> Lord, I have so much going on today. I **need** to talk with you.
> When it comes to my kids, I clearly need your patience,
>   Lord. I have none.
> Help me to work as hard as I can on this project and leave
>   the results to you.
> Give me perspective on what really matters today.
> Jesus, thank you for simply being with me each day.
> Father, I want to be in constant conversation with you.

Pray without ceasing. Continually. Always. Never stop.[11]

In the midst of our day. In the midst of our week. In the midst of our lives.

Are you far from praying without ceasing? Has it been days, weeks, months, possibly even years since you've talked with God? Don't be discouraged. I know I feel ashamed when my prayer life has been less than it should be. Guilt creeps in because I don't pray. Then I feel like I shouldn't pray, like I'm disqualified. If anyone should have the perfect prayer life, it should be a pastor, right? Yet I'm a work in progress.

Instead of being discouraged or feeling disqualified, start talking with God today. Better yet, put this book down and talk with God right now. He's not looking to scold you. He's just so glad to talk with you. He delights in you. Whenever you start talking with God, he's glad to be with you, as any good father would be.

––––––––

Between years in college, I came home and worked two summers for my dad.[12] My dad is retired now, but for most of his life he was an electrician. Some of my favorite memories with my dad come from those two summers.

While wiring a new house, we'd sit on five-gallon buckets turned upside down. Drilling holes. Pulling wires. Hanging light fixtures. Putting in outlets. As we worked, even in the midst of a jam-packed day, we would talk, and talk, and talk some more, the entire day.

I heard stories about my dad that I had never heard before.[13] He was patient and quick to instruct me if I needed guidance on the work. If I accidentally mixed up wires, he'd gently correct me. And we talked about my hopes. We talked about decisions I was trying to make. We talked through things I was nervous about. Bec and I had recently started dating, and Dad and I talked about that as well. We talked about life.

All day. Every day. All summer. We pretty much talked about everything. I came to know my dad in a way I hadn't known him before. Over those couple of summers, I came to love my dad even more than I already did.

It's not that every day was exciting. That summer there were some days I didn't feel like doing a thing. Some mornings I just wanted to sleep in. My bed felt so good. It was summer break, after all. Yet once I got to work, I couldn't wait for the conversations I would have with my dad. I loved every minute of talking with him. Looking back, I can see that he enjoyed it as much as I did.

It's cool to think about this on an infinite level when it comes to God and talking with him. If you happen to be an electrician, you can speak to God even while drilling holes and pulling wires. If you're running at the gym or mowing the lawn, you can speak to him. About anything. About things weighing on your heart. About decisions you're trying to make. About feeling overwhelmed. About your longings and desires. You can ask him for guidance and instruction on whatever you're facing within a day.

Regardless of what a day holds, we can come to know and understand the heart of God on levels we've never known before. In the midst of the craziest of days, we can fall more in love with him. Simply by talking with him.

And so the question is no longer, *How can I find time to pray?* It's, *How can I make it through this day without praying?*

Once more, pray without ceasing? No question!

How can I not? I want to. I need to. I mean, have I mentioned where I live?

6

Bad driver.

Prayer, then, is primarily and fundamentally surrender ... into the hands of God.

—E. Stanley Jones

Last summer our family went to the greatest place on earth—Walt Disney World.[1] The land of tired parents, thousands of tourists, selfie sticks, and endless walking.[2] I mean, the land of Mickey Mouse, smiles, and where all kids' dreams come true. Greatest place on earth!

My two oldest sons were excited about the Tomorrowland Speedway, a ride advertised as "the roar of mini gas-powered sports cars and the smell of exhaust fumes."

Awesome, right?

The Tomorrowland Speedway has race cars that you drive around the track. The cars are guided by a rail underneath, but the driver has some freedom to steer left or right as the car goes. My boys were pumped. Though they barely made the height requirement for the ride, with an adult riding shot-gun, they could drive the car themselves. My wife hopped into a car with our oldest, and I hopped into the passenger seat of another while my middle son, Wilson, climbed in the driver's side. I said a little prayer to myself and quietly sang, "Jesus take the wheel." Wilson was smiling ear to ear, and the "smell of exhaust fumes" was definitely in the air. We were ready!

A few insights on my son Wilson. He has the gift of stubbornness, and he's also a scrappy fighter. He will figure things out on his own and do things his way. He knows exactly what he wants and likes being in control. He also knows what's best for him—or so he thinks—and no matter what, he'll do what he wants.

The light turned green, and I pushed the gas because Wilson's legs wouldn't reach the pedal. And we were off! Well, kind of. Remember the rail under the car and the freedom to turn left and right? Seconds into the ride we were forcefully thrown back and forth in the car. One second Wilson would turn sharply to the left, and we'd be jerked to the right. The next second he'd overcorrect right, and we'd be jerked left. We were barely moving forward, but we were being tossed around like rag dolls. Between the smell of exhaust fumes, slight dehydration from a full day of walking around the most magical place on earth, and the rough ride, my eyes and head were spinning.

I finally grabbed the wheel.

Though his pride was shaken, I could tell that Wilson was relieved that I did. We began to cruise around the track, the wind blowing through our hair. It was great! This is what Tomorrowland is all about.

But once more, stubborn and scrappy, Wilson asked if he could take the wheel again. I said yes, and from the moment Wilson grabbed it, we were back to violently ping-ponging from side to side. Left. Then right. Then left. Right. Left. As the seat belt dug into me, I wondered if I might end up dying on a ride meant for little kids at the greatest place on earth.

Seconds into driving again, this time with zero hesitation or reservation, not caring what his older brother would say when the ride was done, Wilson began to shout, "Dad, you drive! You drive, Dad!"

He didn't want to drive anymore.

He didn't want to be in control.

He didn't want to do his thing.

He didn't even want to help.

Wilson was a terrible driver.[3] I knew it. And so did he.

———

When I look back at most of my prayers and the things I've said to God, it's a lot of my telling him what I need and then asking him to provide it. It's me laying out my requests and asking him to grant them.

Lord, help me get into this college.

God, help this girl to like me.

Lord, help me get this job.

God, make it possible for us to buy this house.

Let the weather on Saturday be perfect.

Jesus, help me win the lottery. It doesn't hurt to ask, right?

Basically, I want, I want, I want.

Like my son Wilson, I'm stubborn and scrappy. I think I know exactly what I need. I want to figure things out on my own. I like being in control. I think I know what's best for me. I am an adult, after all.

So my prayers often look like this:

God, please do _____.

God, help me to _____.

God, I want _____.

God, I need _____.

———

Just to be clear: we have a heavenly Father who *loves* to hear our requests. He loves to provide for us. There is nothing too big or too small to ask for. He wants us to come to him. He wants to hear our needs. I'm always amazed by the way God is in even the smallest details. Jesus himself actually told us to ask things of God.

"Ask, and you will receive."

"For everyone who asks, receives."

"Your heavenly Father gives good things to those who ask him."[4]

And though God tells us we can ask for anything, that doesn't mean he will give it to us every time. Thank God for that, right? Garth Brooks wasn't joking when he said that "some of God's greatest gifts are unanswered prayers."[5]

Here's the reality. When it comes to life, I'm a lot like Wilson: a terrible driver. Horrendous is more like it, and I don't think I'm alone in that.

We tend to be control freaks, don't we? We're control freaks and we also believe we're geniuses. Scroll through Facebook sometime. We know everything! I actually can't believe we still have problems in this world when everyone is so brilliant.

But the truth is that we have little control over anything. And brilliant? We're idiots. Well, at least *I* am. I have no idea what's best for me. When I'm behind the wheel of my life, I'm ping-ponging out of control and my head is spinning. I fight and I hold on to the wheel as long as I possibly can until, finally, the words come out.

Father, you drive.

Lord, you take control.

Jesus, I want to follow you.

God, please do what you think is best.

God, I want what you want.

You drive.

Then a few days will pass—sometimes only a few hours—before I take over driving again, only to find myself immediately tossed back and forth. I hate to admit it, but I'm so stubborn.

When I look back at my life, I see all of the wild rides I endured simply because I wasn't willing to give up control.

Things that I wanted from God.

Things I asked God for.

Things I thought I needed.

Things I was sure I couldn't live without.

Relationships with girls that I wanted to work out, even though it wasn't meant to be. I tried and kept trying.

Opportunities that didn't come together that left me devastated.

Dealing with the stress and worry of life all on my own.

All the while, the best words I could have spoken were these: "God, you drive. You're a better driver than I am. You're in control of the world, and I can't even steer my own life. You're better at knowing what's best for me. You know what I need much better than I do."

It's powerful to look at the words and prayers of Jesus.

We see a picture of what this looks like in the deepest sense.

The night before facing the Cross, Jesus was by himself in a garden. Overwhelmed by what was ahead. He knew he was about to die. And in that moment, we see Jesus pray in anguish: "Not my will but your will must be done."[6]

Even when it made no sense at all. Even in the face of death itself.

Jesus knew that God's ways are better.

His plan is so much better than ours.

———

For the remaining half of Tomorrowland Speedway, Wilson asked me to drive. He didn't "let me" drive. He wanted me to. He asked me to.

We smoothly cruised around the remainder of the track.

Wilson regained his smile.

I regained a calm stomach.

We laughed as I drove. As we parked our car, unbuckled our seat belts, and got out, I asked him, "What did you think?"

"It was awesome, Dad!"

The longer I follow Jesus, the more I find myself praying, *God, what do you want? What do you think I need? What is your plan? What is your will?*

The longer I follow Jesus, the more I find myself asking him to take control. And the more he takes control, the more I get to live into this response— "That was awesome, Dad!"

7

Marathon.

To [pray] for [others] is the most powerful and practical
way in which we can express our love for them.

—John Calvin

I am not a runner.

I like to walk. Walking is good. But running is a different story. You'll never
see me running without a legitimate reason. Like for a Chipotle burrito.[1] I
might "run" to Chipotle for that. In my car.

My wife, on the other hand, loves to run. Weird, I know.

In college, she ran a couple of miles each week for exercise. But after we got
married and the kids showed up, she began running more often and longer.
Maybe to escape us? For her, running is her time to decompress and be
alone. Endorphins became her drug of choice.

When she signed up to run her first marathon, I have to admit I thought she was nuts.[2] "You're *choosing* to run 26.2 miles? Your car isn't broken down? You're not being chased by the Mafia? That's crazy!"

For perspective, a marathon takes about 55,000 steps.

As a supportive husband should, on the day of the marathon, I went along to cheer her on. I dropped Bec off at the starting line, then the kids and I went ahead a few miles. It was my first marathon as well. Watching, that is. Tough work, but someone had to do it. I didn't know what to expect, other than seeing a bunch of people run 55,000 steps.

It ended up being so much more than that. It was powerful. Awesome actually. I didn't expect to be moved like I was. Friends, family, and complete strangers lined the sidelines of the 26.2-mile route and cheered. They yelled. Even screamed. Some shook cowbells as the runners passed by.

"Keep going!"

"You're doing great!"

"You're looking good!"

"Way to go!"

"Keep running!"

"You can do it!"

———

In my brief thirty-five years of living, I've already found that life isn't a fifty-yard dash. It's a lot more like a marathon.

You can't see the finish line.

There are straightaways that get old, seeing the same thing mile after mile.

There are twists and turns in the road. Ups and downs.

There are valleys where you can coast a bit.

And then there are the hills. At times there are even mountains you have to climb.

Sometimes you feel like you could run forever, and other times you're so dog-tired that taking another step seems impossible.

Life is definitely a marathon. All 55,000 steps and then some.

However, there is one big difference between life and an actual marathon.

In life, there aren't always people cheering you on. In life, people aren't always encouraging. When you face a mountain, there may be no one there to say, "Keep going!" Often it's just the opposite. We live in a society with people who are quick to "comment" and post their negative thoughts. Quick to voice a critical opinion of everything and everyone. Quick to bad-mouth. Quick to bring others down, to point out the failures, mistakes, and disappointments of others. Why do we do this?

At times people are hurtful. They're judgmental. They're just plain jerks who are anything but encouraging. This includes followers of Jesus. Sometimes, Christians are even worse. I'm often saddened by how quickly Christians criticize their own brothers and sisters. In the church, we're quick to point fingers, gossip, and judge each other. In my years as a pastor, I've seen many who have left the church and God and never returned because of the gossiping and judgmental attitude of Christians. They know God loves them, but they don't always feel that love from his people.

———

Earlier we looked at Paul's words to a group of Christians in the city of Thessalonica. Reminder: Paul was explaining to them how to live as Christians. He told them to "pray without ceasing." However, a few verses before that, Paul told them, and us, to "encourage one another."[3] More literally, that could be translated as "comfort" or "strengthen" one another.

Encourage your friend.

Comfort your coworker.

Strengthen a neighbor.

This same word—encourage—can also be translated as "pray."[4]

Encourage and pray for your friend. Comfort and pray for your coworker. Strengthen and pray for your neighbor.

Encourage one another by praying for each other. Comfort others by praying for them. Strengthen each other through prayer.

When life is a marathon, is there anything more powerful we can do for each other? In a world that is quick to tear down and discourage, is anything more needed?

More and more, I'm beginning to realize that there is no greater gift that I can receive from friends, family, and even complete strangers than their prayers for me.

I am encouraged by the words and prayers of others.

I am comforted by someone praying for me.

I am supernaturally strengthened by someone talking to God for and about me.

That's powerful stuff.

Again, we're told to "encourage one another."

———

Practically speaking, encouraging others through prayer can look a million different ways.

It can be done while grabbing lunch with a friend. You can ask if there's anything he's going through right now, then pray for him, his needs, his marriage, his health (and maybe the meal) before chowing down. In so doing, you can almost see the person gain strength right before your eyes.

In the Weber household, whenever someone has a birthday, we all gather around that person before going to bed. We each put one hand on him or her, and we pray. It's quite a sight. My daughter is always reluctant to put her hand on her brothers and vice versa. There are giggles. The little one in the center of the circle always smiles from ear to ear. Beaming. It may seem silly to them, but they're encouraged as we pray.

This summer I felt like I was supposed to pray for random people. Strangers. *Okay, God, what are you telling me to do?* I wound up making a four-by-eight-foot sign with the words "Need prayer?" Then I put it in my car and drove to the busiest road in Sioux Falls.[5] I set the sign against the side of my car and sat on a lawn chair beside it. I couldn't have felt more awkward. And for me that's saying a lot. I kept thinking, *There is no way people are going to stop.* But they did.

A college girl stopped on her way to school. "I'm running late for class, and it's my final test of the semester. But when I saw the sign, I felt like I was supposed to stop. Can you pray for me?"

Another person stopped and asked if *he* could pray for *me.* I didn't expect that. The man asked me for specific things he could pray for and then he prayed. I was so encouraged by his simple, heartfelt words.

On another day, I was finishing up, putting the sign back in my car, when a vehicle stopped. A younger lady slowly stepped out. She gently walked over to me and said, "I have MS. A few weeks back, I fell, and since then I've needed to use a cane. It's been difficult. But this morning when I woke up, I was able to walk without a cane again. I'm so thankful and excited. Right now I'm headed to see my doctor, but when I saw your sign, I felt like I needed to stop. I just want to pray and thank God that I can walk today without a cane." Little did she know how much she encouraged me.

Sitting on the side of the road with a sign felt awkward, yet I'm glad I did it. It encouraged me, and I hope it encouraged others.

Throughout a "normal" day, I often pray for people sporadically. Sometimes it's for a stranger I cross paths with at Target or a person who randomly comes to mind on my way to work or before calling it a night. It's a gift to pray for those people and ask God that they have a week filled with joy, that they grow in their walk with the Lord, or that they come to know God's purpose for their lives.

Some folks keep a list of names. Others pray as God reminds them of people throughout the day. I often write a person's name down in my Bible. It reminds me to pray for that person, either for a specific need or just because. Sometimes I pray words of comfort for a relative who's going through a difficult season. Other times I pray words of encouragement for a person who I know has a job interview.

Sometimes I pray for strength for a friend battling cancer.

A few months back, a staff person of Embrace, a young mom who had become well known and well loved by many people within our church, received some of the most difficult news imaginable. After a few weeks of having a cold that wouldn't go away, she went in for tests to see if she had pneumonia. The doctors found something much worse.

Stage 4 lung cancer. Bomb dropped.

I've never seen an entire church so shell-shocked. I've also never seen a family more surrounded, loved, and lifted up in prayer. People wanted to help, wanted to support her, wanted to cheer her on, and they did. But more than that, people began to pray. Among other things, a nonstop chain of prayer began that continues today. There are hundreds, if not thousands, of people consistently and faithfully praying for Shannon; her husband, Dave; and the kids.[6]

When I first spoke with Shannon after the diagnosis, she shared about one of her first PET scans. Forty minutes of lying completely still, not being able to move, while holding her arms above her head. It was extremely uncomfortable for Shannon due to the cancer. She tried so hard not to cough, even though her lungs were irritated. This is what she later shared:

"As I was lying there, a peace came over me that I couldn't explain. I couldn't help but think about all of the people from all over the country who were praying for me at that exact moment. I was overwhelmed in the best way possible and was reminded that I wasn't alone. God and his people were with me and for me, cheering me on. We all have hard stuff that we face, and this was mine. But I wasn't alone. The calls, texts, e-mails, and words of people praying reminded me of this."

———

Here's one very practical piece of advice about praying for others: if you tell someone you're going to pray for him or her, do it! For years, I struggled with the bad habit of telling people I would pray for them but never getting around to doing so. I would simply forget. So often "I'll pray for you" is something we say when we don't know what else to say. It's something we e-mail people. Something we write in sympathy cards. We type it as a comment on a friend's Facebook post. We're quick to say it but struggle to follow through on it.

I didn't want my words to be hollow, so I made a simple change. Now if I tell someone I am going to pray for him or her, I ask if I can pray right then and there, or else I silently pray as we part ways. There are other ways to act on this. My wife will often set a daily reminder on her phone to pray for a certain person at a specific time so she doesn't forget.

It might feel strange at first, to pray for someone audibly, but it's amazing the impact our words have when talking with God on someone else's behalf.

Encourage. Comfort. Strengthen. Cheer. Pray for one another.

———

I didn't expect watching people run 55,000 steps to become a spiritual experience, but it did. As I said, friends, family, and complete strangers lined the route, and they were cheering. They were yelling. Encouraging the runners as they came by. It was crazy.

For this German-Norwegian Lutheran boy, it took some time to get into the cheering spirit. I'm usually reserved about things like that, especially when I have no idea who I'm cheering for. But at one stop, I was standing at the base of a hill.[7] And right beside me was an older lady who was cheering on all of the runners as they ran past. I mean, like, full-body cheering and yelling. She was into it. No shame.

At first I thought she just knew a lot of the people. This lady must know *everyone*! But it quickly became clear that she didn't know any of them. She was cheering on complete strangers. Anyone who passed by. And she was loud. Like an overzealous mom at a soccer game.

"Keep it going, buddy!"

"You can make it up the hill!"

"You can do it, girl! You've got this!"

"You're running hard. Nice work!"

She was contagious to watch and listen to. After a while, I couldn't resist. I had to try it myself. Quietly at first, as reservedly as I could, I began to cheer.

"Keep going!"

"Nice job!"

"You only have twelve miles left!" Okay, actually I didn't say that one.

After just a few minutes of cheering, I went from speaking softly to shouting. I really got into it, cheering them on like a wild man. I didn't know anyone but my wife, but I hoped my words could help them run. They were strangers, yet I wanted the best for them. I wanted them to get a fresh wind for the miles ahead. I hoped my cheering would spur them on.

Then it hit me. It was as if God spoke, *Adam, this is what church should look like.*

As followers of Jesus, this is what we're called to do for others—anyone we cross paths with. They may not be close friends or even someone we know. But when we see that people are going through a difficult time, we should be quick to cheer them on. Quick to encourage them. We should pray for them. This is what the church should be known for.

I've heard that the hardest part of running a marathon isn't the end. It's the places along the 26.2-mile route, the long stretches within the 55,000 steps, where there is no one along the path cheering. The hardest sections are those where there's no one encouraging the runner to keep going, the stretches where the runner feels all alone. Places where you feel like you could quit running and no one would even notice.

I've found the same is true in life.

———

One of my favorite things to do is to write notes to people. To thank people. To encourage people. To let them know I'm praying for them.[8] I want my notes to have a personal touch, but since my handwriting looks like a first grader's, I type them. Not on a computer. I use a typewriter. I should say typewriters. Let's just say I have a few.[9] I may have an addiction to buying them. Anyway, it's just a simple way to let people know that I'm thinking about them, cheering for them, and praying for them. It's a simple way to let them know that they're loved and noticed by me.

As I'm typing a note, I simply begin praying for the person. "I just want you to know that I prayed for you today . . ."

And I begin to list the specific things that I pray.

"For you."

"For your work."

"For your family."

"For your walk with the Lord."

"For your health."

"For your marriage."

"For decisions you're trying to make."

It's so simple, and yet I never cease to be blown away by the responses I get.

"The timing of your note was perfect. I was waiting for test results."

"You prayed for my marriage, and we just started seeing a counselor."

"I've been struggling with depression, and your words were comforting."

"No one's ever told me that he has prayed for me."

"Lately I've been overwhelmed by life, and your letter was so encouraging."

It's amazing how powerful our words to God can be. How powerful our prayers on behalf of others can be. And even as you read this now, I want you to know that I've prayed for you.

I've prayed that the words in this book would meet you right where you are.

I've prayed that your relationship with God would come more fully alive, whether you're on the fence about God or have been following Jesus for years.

I've prayed that you'd begin to talk with God, that it would be a conversation and not a ritual.

I've prayed that you would know that you are loved by God. That he delights in you. That he loves talking with you.

And I've also prayed that you would begin to pray for and encourage others yourself.

A quick favor: Take a minute to pray for a friend, coworker, or neighbor that you know. Whether you have a typewriter or not, I'd be so grateful if you'd be willing to take the time, even five minutes, to write a note to the person you prayed for and let him or her know that you did. That would make my day, and I know it would make that person's as well. Oh, and also, let me know if I can pray for you or your friend as well. Send me a tweet @adamweber.

———

Not all of us are runners. Some of us may be walkers. But all of us can cheer.

This idea of praying for others on a daily basis may be uncomfortable and awkward at first, just like me trying to cheer at my first marathon. But I've found that the more I do this, the more normal it becomes. I hear a need. I see a friend. I watch a heartbreaking news story on TV. And I take a moment to pray for them.

As followers of Jesus, we're called to . . .

Encourage. Comfort. Strengthen. Pray for one another.

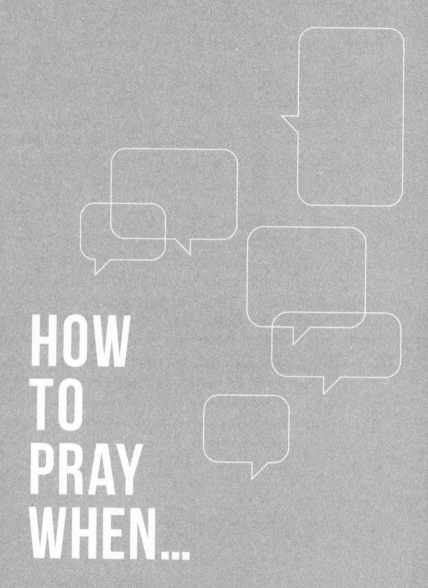

HOW
TO
PRAY
WHEN...

8

You face storms.

The best prayers have often more groans than words.

—John Bunyan

At the first sign of a storm, or even a cloud, there are some people who close all their windows, lock all their doors, and spend the next twenty-four hours in their fully supplied bomb shelter, complete with a small television, a porta-potty, and enough beef jerky and M&M's to last for months.

Then there are others who, when the clouds move in and the weather actually begins to look fairly serious, open their garage door, go outside, and sit on a lawn chair just to watch the action.

I, without question, fall into the second group.[1] If it's hailing, if it's blowing, if a storm is coming directly toward my house, I want to be outside to see it. There's something truly awesome about watching a storm in all of its power and strength, knowing that it can't be controlled or contained.

Once when I was in high school, I stood out in the middle of an alfalfa field with my brother Luke during a violent storm. We saw it coming and couldn't get outside fast enough. We stood in awe as the dark clouds above us churned in circles. Clearly, I wasn't the sharpest kid in my class.

It's a different story though when it comes to the storms we face in life. I mean, I haven't met a person yet who loves those kinds of storms. Not one. Similar to actual storms, life storms can be devastating, bringing damage, pain, and brokenness into our lives. And, like bad weather, they usually show up out of nowhere. When you least expect them. When you're totally unprepared. Storms are outside of our control.

It's amazing how quickly a person's day, a person's *life,* can completely change.

With one phone call. One conversation. An e-mail. A knock at the door. One poor decision—everything can turn in an instant.

The loss of a loved one.

A poor health report.

A rough season.

The end of a relationship.

The loss of a dream.

Unexpected news.

Unwanted transition.

Failure.

There are the storms that we experienced as kids, or the storms we saw our parents weather, that somehow, all these years later, still affect us.

Some storms show up because of someone else's actions and decisions. Because of someone else's junk. Someone else's sin. Someone else's mistake.

And though we hate to admit it, there are other storms that we've brought upon ourselves. By our own actions and decisions. Our own junk. Our own sin. The mistakes we've made.

Storms can hit us in so many different ways, seemingly out of nowhere. And when they do, they leave damage in their wake.

———

On one occasion, Jesus and his disciples got into a boat to cross the Sea of Galilee. And as they were crossing, we're told that a "furious squall came up, and the waves broke over the boat, so that it was nearly swamped."[2]

Just to be clear: This wasn't a storm that you'd want to pull out a lawn chair for and watch. It was terrible. Violent. It can also translate as an "earthquake under the sea." And now their boat was quickly filling with water from the waves.

Thankfully, Jesus was with them, right? Kind of.

Where was Jesus? Sleeping. On a cushion. It was like he brought his favorite memory foam pillow on the trip and was catching a catnap in the middle of this tsunami.

The boat was going to sink, and all the people were probably going to drown, and Jesus was *sleeping*?

I have to be honest. Personally, I find this story confusing, and it only reaffirms something I've often felt. I've been in storms—and I have seen others go through storms—where I've kind of felt like God was, well, sleeping.

Sometimes I've wondered:

How can this be happening?

What is going on here?

How long is this storm going to last?

And better yet:

Where are you, God?

Why aren't you doing anything?

Don't you care?

Lord, are you sleeping *or something?*

———

When I was a senior in high school, I went on my first mission trip to Jamaica. While there, I found out my grandpa had passed away unexpectedly. I was devastated. Here I was on a mission trip for God, and this happened? I couldn't stop crying.

Watching my dad struggle with his health over the past few years has often left me wondering why he has to go through this. He's in constant pain, and a few times he's ended up in the ICU. I grieve every time I see him in such pain, knowing what his life should be versus what it is.

As a pastor, I sometimes think about the miscarriages people in my congregation have suffered or about people dying at a young age. I think about illness. Suicide. Broken marriages. Job losses. I could go on and on and on about people I know whose lives have been left in complete ruin by life's storms.

The first funeral I ever performed was for a young man who took his own life. A police officer called one Saturday morning and asked if I knew him. I did. The officer continued: "Last night, he took his life, and he left a note instructing that you were to be the pastor to do his funeral."

The hardest part was that this was the same young man who had called the day before and asked to get together with me. We met at a picnic table in one of my favorite parks in Sioux Falls. It was a beautiful Friday afternoon, and we talked about nothing outside of the norm. Near the end of our conversation, he asked me, "How can a person know that he is forgiven?" We talked, prayed together, and left. It was no different than countless other conversations I've had with people. A few hours later, however, he took his life.

What? How did I miss that? What could I have said or done differently? Was it my fault? I couldn't breathe. I was devastated. I met with the family a few hours later in the man's home. They cried, and so did I. They felt anger, deep sadness, betrayal. Over the weeks and months that followed, I can't tell you how many times I replayed that conversation in the park in my head. I had nightmares. It was a storm I never saw coming.[3]

You have your own storms and stories as well.

Times of loss.

Moments of heartache.

Something involving your parents. Or your kids. Or siblings. Or spouse. Or a friend. Or yourself.

Storms will, in fact, come.

———

So where was Jesus in the midst of this storm? The disciples hurried to Jesus and woke him up. They cried out to him, "Teacher, don't you care if we drown?"[4]

Then something happened that, if we're not careful, we might gloss over: Jesus got up.

That doesn't sound like much, especially since he'd just been sleeping. Yet it changed everything. It still does.

They cried out. And Jesus heard them.

He heard their words. He heard their cries for help. He didn't ignore them and go back to sleep. He listened to what they had to say.

And he got up.

Could it be that Jesus was actually waiting for the disciples to reach out to him? To ask for his help? To talk with him?

Throughout the Bible, from Exodus to the Psalms to the New Testament, we see this same thing happen. When we speak, when we talk, when we pray, God hears our voices. Specifically, he hears our cries for help.

Listen to these words from the psalmist David: "In my distress I cried out to the LORD; I called to my God for help. God heard my voice from his temple; I called to him for help, and my call reached his ears."[5]

God listens to our voices. He hears our cries for help.

————

As a parent, there are a few things I want my kids to know about God and never forget, whether they need to remember it tomorrow or when they're twenty-five years old and a girlfriend or boyfriend breaks up with them. (Side note: I'm so glad my kids aren't dating until they're twenty-five.)[6]

When my kids have a rough day, or sometimes at night before they go to sleep, I remind them. But more often than not, I remind them in the car as I'm dropping them off for school. Each weekday morning, my two oldest boys ride in the backseat of my blue Chevy Aveo, and each day as I'm driving to school, we talk.[7] We have ten minutes in the car together. Those are ten of my favorite minutes each day. Sometimes we talk about their video games. Sometimes we chat about what Mom packed in their lunch bag. But we often talk about God. And when we talk about God, I remind them of this:

God loves them—no matter what.

God is always with them. There's no place they can go where he isn't already there.

And lastly. That they can cry out to God, and he will hear their voices.

If they're scared, hurting, lonely, or grieving at any time, any place, under any circumstance, they can always talk with God.

That last point, particularly, is so important to me for them to know. Why? Because there have been so many times I've needed to know this and be reminded of it myself. Times that I've simply needed to know that God hears my voice.

———

When my oldest was born, we lived hours away from family. I was a rookie dad, and when it came to the birth of tiny humans, all I knew was that it was supposed to all happen like clockwork. We did the pre-baby classes. We were ready. Just go to the hospital. Labor. Baby comes. Baby cries. Mom holds baby. And there would be nothing to worry about, right? Which was true. Until it actually came time for Hudson's birth.

Becky was at work when her water broke. I picked her up, and we drove to Saint Joseph East hospital in Lexington, Kentucky.[8] All was great until near the end of labor. Hudson's heart rate started going all over the place, and the doctors decided he needed to come out sooner rather than later.

As he was coming out, it became clear that something was terribly wrong. I could see it on the faces of the nurses. Out of nowhere, fifteen different people, doctors and nurses, appeared in the room. The heart monitor was beeping, and Hudson was blue, not making a sound.

Wasn't he supposed to start crying? Then I saw it. The umbilical cord was tightly wrapped around his neck. Instead of handing us our baby to hold, they quickly took him away and a team of people worked frantically to help him breathe.

In that moment, my heart was torn into pieces for someone I had seen for less than a minute. I was scared. And broken.

All I could do was cry out. Literally, I was crying as I prayed. I didn't even think about it. The words just came out from the deepest part of me.

God, are you sleeping?

Is he going to be okay?

Would you be with my new son?

Help him to breathe, Lord.

Father, I'm scared!

If you struggle to "pray," do you know how to yell? Can you scream? Have you ever cried out to God? Shouted at the sky? Shaken your fist in the air? Maybe you've been praying for years and didn't know it.

When we speak. When we talk. When we pray. When we cry out. God hears our voice.

———

Back in the boat, Jesus got up. But there's more: He "rebuked the wind and said to the waves, 'Quiet! Be still!' Then the wind died down and it was completely calm."[9]

Jesus *commands*. He tells the wind and the waves what do to. Crazy, right?

More than just the winds and waves dying down though. The deeper meaning of the word *calm* is about more than the weather, more than the physical storm stopping. It's describing a mysterious, supernatural calmness. A sort of unexplainable stillness and peace.

And don't miss it. When the storm passed, the disciples were no longer talking about the wind and the waves. They didn't mention the storm. Instead, they talked only about Jesus.

"Who is this? Even the wind and the waves obey him!"[10]

Even after the worst of storms, the places in my life that I still ask, "Why?" Even in the places I still don't understand, when the calm finally comes, I too am left talking about Jesus.

———

The night Hudson was born, I cried more than I thought was humanly possible. My eyes hurt because I cried so much. Thankfully, the next morning Hudson was cleared by the nurses and I was able to hold my healthy son. I give thanks for Hudson daily, and I only wish every story ended like this. I wish the storm was calmed every time. Sadly, that's not the case.

What happens when the storms come, we cry out to God, and the worst still takes place? What happens when it feels like God is silent? Like he's sleeping and *doesn't* get up?

Have you been there before? Have you endured a storm that seemed to shake everything, including the foundation of all that you know about God? I without question have been in this place.

Sometimes I don't pray because I question whether it will change anything. Does it really matter if I do? Other times I don't pray because I don't want to be disappointed by God. What if I pray and nothing happens? Will it shake my faith in prayer? Will it shake my belief in God?

For the past five years, my dad has had a pain issue. The pain has completely altered his life. He went from being one of the most active, healthy people I've ever known to lying in bed a majority of each day because of the pain. Mom and Dad now have a bed in their living room so he doesn't have to be alone in the bedroom during the day. He walks with a cane. He is in constant pain. It's horrible.

I can honestly say that I've never prayed more faithfully for anyone in my life. I've prayed for years that he would be healed. On my knees, crying out, yelling at God—I've done it all. I've prayed alone. I've asked others to pray with me. Yet in spite of my cries, Dad's condition has continued to worsen. Even now, I cry just thinking about it. I want so much for him to be healed. I want him not to be in any more pain.

I could attempt to explain the unexplainable. I could offer reasons and explanations to your questions and mine, but at times there simply aren't any. None that satisfy. I've found that trite answers only cause more hurt than good.

When I ask my dad his thoughts on what he's going through, specifically the times his very life has been in jeopardy, he's the first to admit that he has questions too. At times he cries about it. Having had to retire early, he's worried about finances. He worries about my mom being alone if something were to happen to him. Yet he's also quick to say that more than ever before, he realizes that God is truly good, that he's in control of all things, and that he'll provide everything we need. He's realized that even death itself isn't a bad thing.

A few years ago, Dad had surgery and experienced complications afterward. He had to go back into surgery again that same day. Before being wheeled into the operating room for the second time, at one of his worst moments, he asked my mom to play the song "10,000 Reasons" on her cell phone so he could listen to it. It's a song that talks about praising God, and all the reasons we have to thank God, regardless of what we're facing. Matt Redman reminds us that though our days may draw to a close, our souls will still "sing Your praise unending."[11]

I can't say it any better. I guess my dad is choosing to focus on Jesus in the midst of the storm. In the end, isn't that what storms do? They remind us of what's important. They remind us who is in control. They remind us to keep focusing on the main thing—Jesus. And if we keep talking with him through the storm, we might come to understand that he's all we've ever really needed.

───────────

I almost forgot. About Jesus sleeping? He wasn't sleeping because he didn't care about the disciples, or because he's heartless, or because he didn't know about the storm. He cared about the disciples, and he was fully aware of the storm. Jesus was able to sleep because of his complete trust and wholehearted faith in God, his Father. The One who never sleeps. The One who sees everything. The One who is always present. The One who is in control of all things. The One who, even when life makes no sense at all, is able to work all things together for the good of those who love him.

Jesus was in the same storm and the same boat as the disciples. The only difference was his complete trust in God. Because he had such peace, he was able to sleep. In a boat. In the midst of a terrible, furious storm.

Jesus knew without a shadow of doubt that when he talked to his Father, God would hear his voice.

Just like he hears our cries for help today. Thank you, Lord.

Any time. Any place. Under any circumstance. You can cry out to God, and he will hear your voice. If you're scared, hurting, lonely, or grieving. You can always talk with God. No matter the storm that comes your way.

9

You're discouraged.

We have this sense in our gut that we are created
to have some kind of relationship with God.

—Tom Holladay

Something I've noticed lately is that I talk to myself fairly often. Is that weird? Some people call it being slightly crazy. I chalk it up to being an external processor.

I often talk to myself while watching football on television. I'm a Cincinnati Bengals fan[1], and in case you didn't know, they haven't won a single play-off game in more than twenty-five years.[2] Since I was six years old. So typically, I say things like:

"Why am I still cheering for this team?"

"They're never going to make it to another Super Bowl."

"I love this team. I hate this team. I love this team . . ."

"Does God have something against the Bengals?"

I'll also talk to myself at the end of a day, just to decompress. Sometimes it's just helpful to talk it out with someone. Or myself.

"Adam, what in the world were you thinking earlier?"

"Why did we decide to have four kids?"

"Tomorrow's a new day! Go get it tomorrow, champ!"

"You look better without hair! Think Bruce Willis. Or the great Andre Agassi." #baldisbeautiful

"I'm good enough. I'm smart enough. And doggone it, people like me."

If I'm mad at someone, I'll talk to myself, usually dreaming about what I would say to the other person. Air punching him in the face. Only kidding. I just quote Bible verses about the wrath of God.

There are times I'll laugh out loud at my own lame jokes. True story! Is that bad?

It's not as weird as it seems, and I do have friends, by the way. Haven't you caught yourself talking to yourself? I hope I'm not the only one.

———

One of the best-known psalms in the Bible is Psalm 42. It was written by David. We're not told what David was going through at the time, so we're not sure exactly what all happened to him. But it's quite clear that David was experiencing a low point. He was struggling with something.

And what did David say? At two different points in this psalm, he talked to himself. (See, I'm not crazy. It's in the Bible!) Here's what David says:[3]

> *Why are you downcast, my soul? And why so disturbed within me?*

A few verses later, David again says the same exact thing. Basically asking himself,

> *Why am I so discouraged?*

> *I don't understand . . . why do I feel this way?*

> *Why is my soul so restless?*

> *Why am I so sad?*

> *Why am I so troubled on the inside?*

I'm guessing that at some point, we've all felt this way and we've all talked to ourselves. Whether it was aloud or just in our heads, we've asked ourselves questions like,

> *Why am I struggling like this?*

And why am I so restless?

Why am I thinking this way?

Why do I feel so empty?

Now, there are certain times when it's natural to feel this way. When we're going through a trial, like struggling to get pregnant or dealing with a broken relationship, it's natural to struggle internally.

When we've experienced a loss, something major like the loss of a parent or something less vital but still impactful like the loss of the family's golden retriever, it's natural to feel sad or empty.

During times of transition, when moving to a different city, after accepting a different job, when finding out you no longer have a job—it's natural to feel uncertain at times like these.

But I've also found myself feeling this way when life is going pretty well. Sometimes my soul feels restless when my life is fantastic and there's really nothing to complain about.

In these moments, I actually begin to feel even worse. On an even deeper level, I start thinking,

> *My life is so good; why am I not happy?*
> *I have everything I could ever want and need. Why am I feeling this way?*
> *I don't understand why my emotions are all over the place.*

I don't know why I'm struggling.
I have nothing to worry about: why am I so
*   anxious?*
Why do I feel so empty?
How come I'm never satisfied?
Am I going off the deep end?

A bit more about David. He was one of the most beloved kings who ever lived. Wealthy. A hero who courageously killed a giant. "A man after [God's] own heart."[4] If anyone should have had his act together, if anyone should have had life figured out, it'd be David. Yet he didn't. Something was still missing. In some strange way, that's encouraging to me.[5]

Just like David, even when things are pretty good, we often come to a place where we start talking to ourselves. We ask questions like,

Why are you downcast, my soul?
And why so disturbed within me?

And if this sounds familiar, know you are not alone. Almost weekly, people will come up to me after a church service and ask me versions of the same questions.

"I have everything. A nice house. A beautiful family. Money. A good job. And yet it just feels like something is missing in my life. What's wrong with me?"

It's like they got the American dream.

They reached their goal.

They got what they had been chasing for years.

They got married.

They were promoted.

They finally got _____.

Then they realized that what they wanted didn't deliver what it had promised.

It didn't give peace, wholeness, joy, love, or life. It didn't satisfy their souls like they hoped it would.

Now what?

————

So David was talking to himself, and he asked these questions of why he felt this way and why he was so discouraged. And yet, surprisingly enough, all throughout the psalm, David actually answered his own questions. His answer?

As the deer longs for streams of water so my soul longs for
you, O God.
My soul thirsts for God, the living God.[6]

David declared to God, and he reminded himself, that in his restlessness, what he really longed for was God.

Lord, I want and I need more of you.

When it comes to my soul, only one thing calms it; only one thing satisfies it.

Only one thing is enough and gives me peace. The only thing that makes me whole is you!

Without you, God, even on the best of days, I'm restless.

Without you, Lord, even when I have everything, I actually have nothing.

Without you, Father, I'm empty. I'm broken. I'm discouraged. I'm anxious.

I feel like I'm losing my mind.

My soul and your soul. They long for and they thirst for God.

What's crazy is that, just like David, we'll often try anything and everything this world has to offer to satisfy this feeling before discovering the truth. We try to fill our soul's longing through a job or career. We think that maybe if we can just get the next promotion or a different job or that award, it'll be enough.

We try relationships and sex. Maybe we're with the wrong person, we think, so we try to see if someone else can satisfy us. Maybe we just want someone to give us a little more attention, even if it's only for one night, and we wake up with regret the next morning. Or we're so lonely or so sick of being single that we date someone we know we shouldn't. *If I just had someone, anyone, then my life would be complete.*

We try money and material things. If we could just get a bigger house or nicer place, we'd be happy. If we just had more money and a new car and a boat and the ability to take that vacation. We know it sounds shallow, but we think that if we just had the newest phone or that pair of shoes, then life would be great.

We'll try everything to fill this need. Status. Success. Drugs. Porn. Power. Enhancing our appearance and health. Earning another degree. Gaining more followers on Twitter or Instagram. Having kids. Having hobbies.

Yet it never ever seems to be enough. If it were, we'd stop searching. If it were enough, we wouldn't be consumed with wanting more.

Like David, we find out that it's not enough. It leaves our souls downcast. So we keep hoping that the next thing will do it. The next thing will satisfy us. The next thing will be enough. Yet, it never is.

And when we come to this realization that more isn't enough, it becomes clear that David was on to something. Only God can satisfy the longing of our souls. Only he can give us peace. Only he can make us whole.

————

To this day, I don't have an equation to prove God's existence. I wish I did. The skeptic in me wishes I had hard facts. But for me, this feeling inside of us, this longing for God, this thirst for him is one of the main things that leads to my belief in him. It is the closest thing I have to proof. When I have doubts, I come back to this. No matter how hard I try, I can't deny the longing within myself. And I haven't met a person yet who doesn't feel this restlessness for something greater. We seem to have an aching within us that we can't satisfy. Without God, something is missing within our soul. We are restless.

I often sense this restlessness at night.

I'm a bit of a night owl, especially now that we have kids. It seems like that time right before going to bed is the only time I have when it's truly quiet. No one is screaming. No one is running naked through the house. All is calm. All is bright. Just like the night Jesus was born. Angels are singing. *Thank you, God!*

It's in that time of quiet that I either sense God's presence, because I've been talking with him and have included him in my thoughts throughout the day, or I clearly sense my need for him. I clearly sense that something is missing.

Why? Because God hasn't been a part of my day, maybe even my week. I feel nutty because I haven't talked with him. I've managed to stay busy enough that I didn't feel this need sooner.

But when I finally slow down. When I'm quiet. When I'm still for even five seconds. It's then that I get this overwhelming sense of my need for Jesus, my need to talk with him. This is the longing, the thirst.

———

And to be clear, God isn't just enough. He's *more* than enough.

He doesn't want us simply to stop being restless. He wants us to know a peace that surpasses all understanding.

He doesn't only want us to go through life feeling "not discouraged." He wants our lives to overflow with joy.

He doesn't just want us to avoid feelings of insecurity about our identity. He wants us to know his love for us, which is beyond measure.

We have a God who is more than enough.

And, personally, I can feel it right away when I'm trying to make it through a day on my own. I can sense it within my soul when I haven't talked with God. I can tell almost immediately. The moment that I'm not close to him.

How? Because it's the same moment I start talking to myself.

10

You're stuck in the mud.

Talk to God as a child talks to his father,
asking Him for what we want.

—Charles Spurgeon

To a second grader, mud is one of the greatest things ever—to walk in, to play with, to throw at your little brother. It's all fun and games though until you're so stuck in the mud you literally can't move.

A few years ago, my family and some family friends went to see the progress on the construction of our lake cabin.[1] It was a wet, cold spring day, and we decided to pack up the kids and make the hour-and-a-half drive. My brother-in-law was putting up the walls on the cabin, and we were pumped about being able to use it that coming summer.

Weeks earlier, the foundation had been excavated, and we had a small mountain of dirt to prove it. We arrived to find that the South Dakota spring, mixed with a particularly wet day, had turned our mountain of dirt into a mountain of mud. It was Mud Everest!

Before we got out of the van, we warned our kids to steer clear of the mountain. "You can play anywhere else, but don't get anywhere close to that pile of mud," we told them. I felt like God talking with Adam and Eve: "You can eat the fruit from any tree but that one!" The mud was thick and messy. If the kids wandered into it, they would get covered with it head to toe. And we didn't have any changes of clothes.

Our cabin sits on two acres of land, which feels like a small country to our city kids. There's wildlife—deer, pheasants, and plenty of gophers. There's also a lake for skipping stones and catching fish. It's paradise for a group of kids. So on that day, there was only one guideline: "You can play anywhere else except the mud. Go and explore!"

Excited to be there, we slid open the doors on our minivan, and we all piled out. I began to show our friends the cabin, explaining the layout and our plan to make it a small resort haven.

We were only a few minutes into the short but grand tour when I heard, "Daddy! Daddy! I'm stuck!"

I heard the scream and went running. Was someone hurt? Sixty different questions flashed through my parental mind. As I rounded the corner of the cabin, I found my oldest son absolutely covered in mud. Crying. He was powerless and embarrassed. And he was standing knee-deep in mud. He pleaded with me to come pull him out. He was stuck!

———

For some reason, we are all drawn to mud, aren't we? Like kids to literal mud, human beings in general are drawn to the things that leave us powerless, embarrassed, and stuck. I'm not sure what it is about us, but it's proven itself true time and time again. We can be standing in the middle of Paradise, yet if we're told to steer clear of just one thing, we're enticed by it all the more. We run right to it. We arrogantly think we can handle it. We can manage life and the consequences of our decisions on our own. Disregarding all the warning signs, we think we know what's best, what will bring us true happiness, fulfillment, and joy. We report to no one. We can do as we please. We can play in the mud if we'd like to, and we think it's harmless. *How bad can it be?* Once again, it's all fun and games. Until we're stuck.

One of the unique things about my job is that I often speak with people at their very worst. When they're standing knee-deep in mud, spiritually speaking.[2]

Someone who's struggling with porn.

A wife caught cheating on her husband.

A man who's been lying and can't seem to get out of the lies.

A young girl who's pregnant and her parents don't know it yet.

A husband with financial secrets.

A twentysomething who can't stop gambling.

As they walk into my office, they're embarrassed. You can see it in their posture. They're broken. Their eyes look down to the ground. They're quiet and slow to speak. They knew that the thing they were drawn to wasn't right, yet they did it anyway. They thought they could handle it and never imagined that it would come to this point. Heads down, they're ashamed. And they're stuck.

———

When my eyes caught my son's that day at the lake house, I didn't need to point out his wrong. He knew it full well. I didn't need to tell him, "I told you so." I didn't need to tell him that what he did was wrong. He knew what he did. He was stuck and pleading for help.

In the Bible we see that King David had some mistakes of his own. An affair. A murder. The guy definitely found his way into some pretty deep mud-holes. In Psalm 40, David wrote these words:

> He leaned down to me;
> he listened to my cry for help.
> He lifted me out of the pit of death,
> out of the mud and filth,
> and set my feet on solid rock.
> He steadied my legs.
> He put a new song in my mouth,
> a song of praise for our God.[3]

Such a powerful picture, isn't it?

God leans down and listens to our cries for help.

Even when we are at our worst, he hears our prayers. Even when we're at the bottom, he hears our words.

Instead of scolding us and telling us to clean ourselves up, making us feel more rotten than we already do, God immediately lifts us out of the pit. Out of the mud. He sets our feet on a new path. He steadies our legs and puts a new song in our mouths.

It's pretty crazy. Even when we dig a pit with our own two hands, fill it with mud, and jump in, God comes and pulls us out. He cleans us up. And he sets us back on solid ground.

He offers us grace. He forgives us of our sin. He makes us new again.

This is true for you. And it's true for me. Every single time.

And yet . . .

What's often our first reaction when we find ourselves stuck in the mud? It's to get ourselves unstuck, right? Instead of immediately calling out to God our Father, we try relentlessly to free ourselves.

I got myself into this mess, we think, *and I have to get myself out.*

Instead of calling out to ask for God's help, we convince ourselves that we should clean ourselves up first. Even if it's just a little bit. Instead of admitting our wrongs, we try to see if there's any way out of the situation. And when we do this, we only make things worse. On our own, when we try to get unstuck from mud, we sink deeper. The same is true with sin.

As my friend and I tried to pull my son out of the mountain of mud, it was clear that before he screamed for help, he had been trying to get free on his own, losing both of his boots in the process. He was standing knee-deep in mud, in his socks.

It's easy to see my son's mistake. It's always easier to see when others are stuck though. Isn't it? It's always easier to see someone else's mistakes. But have you ever been stuck in the mud yourself? I still have flashbacks to the day a teacher caught me cheating on homework in high school. And to the times in college when my relationships with girls weren't what they should have been. Even now there are days when I'm tempted to blur the lines between right and wrong. Maybe you're stuck right now?

It's not a fun place to be. You feel exposed and vulnerable. You feel foolish and embarrassed. Like a kid who avoids her parents after she's done something wrong, you avoid God. You question whether or not he'll forgive you. You struggle to forgive yourself. Everything and everyone tries to convince you that you can't ask for help. You wonder if you've lost your right to pray. You think you have to figure it out on your own.[4]

Instead of avoiding God when we're stuck, however, we should run to him. He should be the very first place we go! The first person we ask for help.

Even at our worst, God hears our prayers. Even at the bottom, he hears our words.

I met Mike when he was forty-eight years old. He had lived a rough life, spending time in prison, battling addiction, cutting off relationships with his family. Just by looking at him, you could tell the guy had been around the block a few times. He was a person who was easy to overlook and easy to want to walk away from.

A couple of years ago, someone invited Mike to our church, and he started attending regularly. Even in the middle of winter, Mike would ride his bicycle miles across town to get there. He didn't miss church.

I got to know Mike. Sometimes during my nightly walks downtown, I'd see him out riding his bike. Whenever he'd see me, he'd peddle over, get off his bike, and start walking with me.

We talked. Sometimes for two minutes. Sometimes for thirty. Each time, he thanked me for talking and rode away.

One Sunday after church, Mike was on his bike heading home when he decided it was time to get baptized. He turned around and came back to church. I've never seen someone more excited about being baptized than Mike was. In that moment, it was as if he finally realized that even he, with his brokenness and imperfections and shortcomings, could have a fresh start at life. In spite of his past mistakes and sin, he could call out and God would hear his voice. God would rescue him.

The last Sunday Mike attended Embrace, he brought a guy with him that he'd met at Dollar General. Mike told the guy that he should come check out the church that changed his life and hear about the God he loves.

Mike unexpectedly passed away shortly after the service. Only God knows the eternal impact that Mike may have had on that man. It's bittersweet in the fullest sense.

Like Mike, we all have a story. We've all made mistakes. Also, just like Mike, it's never too late for us to begin following Jesus. It's never too late to ask for help. And when we do, God will hear our voices.

———

As Hudson stood in Mud Everest, my friend and I reached out our arms. We got ahold of him and pulled. His legs were stuck in the mud, so we pulled even harder. After we finally managed to get him out, through his tears and apologies, I reassured Hudson that it was okay. We pulled his clothes off, sprayed him with water, and wrapped him in a towel. He was relieved, completely humbled, and didn't want to leave my side.

When we're stuck, we are convinced that we can't go to God. We think we have to pull ourselves out of the mud. But the opposite is true. We can be freed, pulled out, and cleaned head to toe, only when we realize our need for God. Freedom starts with realizing that God's ways are much better than ours. And it all starts in prayer, simply by uttering the words:

Daddy, I'm stuck!
Can you help me?
Lord, pull me out of the mess I've gotten myself into.
Forgive me.
Jesus, give me a fresh start.
Father, please make me new.

Here's the truth about that day at the cabin: I didn't say, or even think, a word about Hudson's actions. I spoke only of my love for him and the fact that it hadn't changed. He was and is my son. I loved him then more than ever.

Yes, he was a bit muddy, but it wasn't anything I couldn't handle.

I'll pull him out again, and again, if he ever finds himself stuck.

11

You're exhausted.

We must lay before Him what is in us,
not what ought to be in us.

—C. S. Lewis

"I'm the last person who ever thought he'd be a pastor."

These are typically the first words I say to someone after I'm asked what I do for a living. It's my response partly because I'm the last person who ever thought I'd be a Christian. But mostly it's because, even after ten years of being a pastor, I still don't feel like one.

When I picture a pastor, I envision a person wearing a robe. Someone who speaks using parables and fancy words. Who carries a shepherd's staff and is the picture of peace, stillness, and rest. A person who moves throughout his day at a slow, steady pace.

I, on the other hand, am naturally antsy. Restless is probably more accurate.

I struggle to sit still for longer than a minute or two.[1] I'm always on the go. I pace in circles a lot. I often hear my wife say, "You don't relax very well."

Confession: One of the first things I do when I get home each day is a once-over on the house, tidying everything up. #neatfreak. I've done this since I was a little kid. My Grandma Dahle would tell me, "You are going to make the best husband ever, Adam."[2] I just have to say, my wife might disagree with her. I truly can't sit still; I'm always moving.

My dad is the same way. When I was a kid, it wasn't unusual for me to wake up early on a Saturday morning and find my dad already up, fixing something on the roof or building something in the garage.[3] Just because.

I'm constantly going, moving, or thinking about the next thing. I'm the exact opposite of a still and relaxed person.

Most days, I don't feel anything like a pastor.

––––––

I became a pastor and started Embrace when I was twenty-four years old. It wasn't my idea. I had no desire for or intention of starting a church, but there I was. I was available and God had a plan. We sent a couple e-mails to see if anyone might be interested in coming to a meeting to hear about the possibility of starting a new church. And sure enough, people came that first night.[4]

To start, we decided to worship one time a month. Bec and I were still living in Kentucky, and I was going into my third and final year of seminary.[5] So once a month, I flew back to Sioux Falls for the service, preached, and the next day flew back to Kentucky. Each time I did, I thought it was completely crazy. What were we thinking? Did I mention that this wasn't my idea?

We started with thirty-two people and, within months, grew to around a hundred. Our family moved back to South Dakota, and we switched to weekly services. However, a hundred people is the size we would stay for three years. During those first three years, I tried everything to grow the attendance. Everything. Late nights. Long hours. Stepping out of my comfort zone daily. Using every opportunity to meet and invite someone to church. I knew that if we wanted to keep our doors open, we needed to grow.

For the first three years, we met at another church's building. That church worshipped in the mornings and our church worshipped on Sunday evenings. Around noon each Sunday, we were allowed to put out a large A-frame sign near the road that read "Embrace Church." It took two large men to move it. Then we'd set up the inside of the church building to make it feel like Embrace. We'd worship, and after everyone left, the volunteers and I would put all of Embrace's stuff back into our small storage closet. I had the best volunteers, but we often forgot about the large A-frame sign. Each time we did, I would try to find a friend who could help me move the sign, or I would have to move it on my own.

There was a particular winter night that I won't forget. A snowstorm had come through, but even with a fresh foot of snow on the ground, we still had worship. (Yes, we're hard-core in South Dakota. It can be forty degrees below zero with zero visibility and we'll still have church!) We had the service and then put everything away and we all went home. I drove slowly because of the snow and got all the way to my house before realizing the A-frame sign was still out. I was completely spent and it was late, but it needed to be moved. So I slowly drove back across town through the snow.

I crawled underneath the sign and began to lift it with my shoulders, carrying the sign as I walked through nearly three feet of snow. I was done! That night I hit my first breaking point.

I had only recently completed my master's degree, I didn't want to start this church in the first place, it was struggling to grow, and here I was moving this stupid sign through three feet of snow. Without thinking, the words came out:

God, what am I doing here?
I'm tired!
Why did we start this church in the first place?
I don't want to be here!

The first three years of the church were three of the hardest years of my life.

A few months later, the church changed locations and our service time went from Sunday evenings to Sunday mornings. That first Sunday morning, we thought more people might come, but we never expected what would happen by making this one decision. We doubled in size. Doubled. In a single day. We couldn't believe it.[6]

Each week thereafter, more people showed up.

At first, it was surreal and exciting. After three difficult years, it was finally "working." The church was growing. People were coming. Months passed, and we were still growing at a rapid pace. We had become one of the fastest-growing churches in the country. So fast, I couldn't keep up. So I worked harder and longer. I spent every waking moment trying to figure out how we could keep up with the steady stream of people who were coming.

It seemed that everyone wanted to meet with me for coffee. I couldn't keep up with all the e-mail. I had a wedding to perform almost every weekend. One weekend I married three different couples. The church's phone number was my cell phone. And all the while I was trying to be a husband and a dad. I was dropping balls left and right, and people were getting frustrated.

As a lifelong people pleaser, I couldn't say no. Nothing felt worse than disappointing people, but I was wearing myself to the ground. I was saying yes to everything, and it was quickly taking a toll on me.

The church's rapid growth probably seems like the best-case scenario for any church, but the growth came with so many challenges.[7] Things we had never encountered before. We needed more staff. The level of external criticism increased. People I had never met were scrutinizing our growth.

"Why are they growing so fast?"

"It must be shallow."

"They're all about numbers."

Did I mention that I never wanted to start a church?

First it was three years of struggling to grow. Then overnight it became three years of struggling to keep up. It was all too much.

One night we had a leadership meeting at our church, with ten or so of us there. These people had become some of my closest friends. People I loved and trusted. Before the meeting started, someone asked me how I was doing. I didn't respond. I just started sobbing. Uncontrollably. Tears that I had done so well at keeping to myself came rushing out. After six years of running, running, and running some more, I was burned out.

I was exhausted.

For me, the exhaustion came from six years of pastoring a church. For others, it's caused by having a difficult marriage and continuing to love someone who's hard to love. Or it's parenting a child who seems to make every wrong turn in life. Or it's trying to get a business off the ground. Or making it through college or grad school. Or trying to enjoy your single years after you watch a majority of your friends get married. Or it's trying to get your head above water financially. Or trying to get healthy following setback after setback.

I'm not talking about having a busy week or even a busy season. This is more than merely living in Crazytown. It's burning the candle at both ends for years. I'm talking complete and utter exhaustion.

———

I never would have considered myself a prideful person because I usually struggle with insecurity. But looking back, it was clear that I was prideful and fully self-sufficient.

It's strange. In seminary, I heard the stats on how many pastors leave ministry after three years because of burnout and exhaustion. "Half of you in this room won't be pastors in ten years." Yada yada. It always went in one ear and out the other. I arrogantly thought that must happen to people who don't know how to work hard. People who are soft. But not me. I would be just fine. My wife thinks I'm the hottest, smartest, and strongest man God ever created! (Right, honey?)

Without even knowing it, over the six years, whenever I had faced an obstacle or encountered something I didn't know how to do, I had relied solely on myself. Instead of asking for God's help, instead of reaching out to him, instead of realizing my utter need for him, I put my head down and worked harder. I had convinced myself that I could figure it out. I foolishly believed I could do it on my own.

Looking back, I realized I was pastoring and leading a church—completely out of my own strength and abilities. I had pushed and pushed for years; my life, my words, actions, relationships, and even my soul showed it. I couldn't do it anymore.

My sobfest at the leadership meeting made it clear that something needed to change, or I would become one of the statistics. One more former pastor.

———

In the gospel of Matthew, Jesus invites us, "Come to me, all you who are weary."[8] The word translated "weary" can also mean "tired," or better yet, "exhausted."

Jesus was speaking with a group of his followers and he said, "Are you weary, tired, or exhausted? Come to me, and you will find rest."

Even more so, he tells us, "You will find rest for your souls."[9]

What's a soul? Our soul is the deepest part of who we are. It's what makes you *you* and me *me.* When your entire being is exhausted from working nonstop, it's your soul that needs to find rest.

Our souls long to be refreshed. Where? The only place we can go to find rest—Jesus.

Maybe you've heard this verse before, as it's a classic verse from Jesus. These are words that I'd preached on. Verses that I could easily have recited off the cuff. However, it was a reality I didn't know for myself and hadn't experienced in six years.

I actually told my wife during that season that it felt almost like I didn't have a soul anymore. It was gone. I felt empty. Like a shell of my former self.

————

I began to long for rest, this supernatural rest Jesus talked about. I longed for my soul to be refreshed and could clearly see my utter and complete need for him and the rest he spoke of.

Over the few months that followed, I began to ask God for help. I began going for walks at night as a way to get some fresh air at the end of a day and connect with God. Once Bec and the kids were sleeping, I headed out for forty-five minutes. I walked down the sidewalks under the glowing streetlights with my hands in my pockets. I walked from one block to the next. I talked with God and prayed as I walked. I shared my heart with him. I asked for his rest. I longed for my soul to be refreshed. After my walk, I returned home and went to bed.

My simple daily prayer became *Lord, I need your help.*

Some days it was all I could say. *Lord, I need your help.*

I said it in the morning. *Lord, I need your help.*

I said it multiple times throughout each day. *Lord, I need your help.*

I whispered it to God before going to sleep. *Lord, I need your help.*

Thankfully, God specializes in bringing dead things back to life. Over those months, God took my soul—my burned-out, exhausted soul—and slowly but surely gave it rest. He breathed life back into me. I began to feel again. I began to care again. I began to live again. And it was all because I made the time to talk with him and take him at his promise: "You will find rest."

This promise from Jesus was no longer just a verse I quoted as a pastor. It was no longer just the basis of a message I would share for others. It became a reality within the deepest part of me, within the deepest part of my rested soul.

During this season, one of the hardest things for me to realize was that I'm not invincible. As humans, we pride ourselves on how much we can do and how busy our lives are. The most common answer you'll hear when you ask people how they're doing is a single word: "Busy!" Sometimes they repeat it to show how chaotic their life is. "Busy, busy, busy!"

I used to see being a workaholic as a badge of honor. Sometimes I still believe that one of my best traits is the ability to work nonstop. And yet, it's clear: I'm not a robot. I'm a human with a soul. I can't do this on my own, and I no longer want to try. I'm a person. I'm a pastor in need of Jesus just as much as anyone else, maybe even more.

You're a person too. You have a soul. And you need rest. Even Jesus took time to rest! He took time to be still. To be alone and talk with God.[10]

After that exhausting six-year season, I made some hard changes that were long overdue. We got a separate phone number for the church. I learned how to delegate. Instead of working harder, I started working smarter. Once home I put my phone away. I actually began to take days off. For me that's every Friday. These changes were not easy to make.[11]

A theme and a command found throughout the Bible is the importance of taking a Sabbath. That means taking a day to set work aside. A day to connect with God and others. A day to remind ourselves that God is God and we are not. A day to be renewed, doing whatever renews us.[12] In the 24/7, always connected, constantly available world we live in, I might argue that this is one of the hardest commands in the entire Bible to follow. Especially for someone like me who doesn't have an off switch. Why is it so hard? Because I often believe the lie that I'm in control of things that I'm really not in control of.

———

Now that I'm on the other side of sheer exhaustion, I still find myself tempted weekly, sometimes daily, to do things all on my own. I want to put my head down and work harder. I think I can figure everything out on my own. I try to push and push and push some more. Once I come to my senses, I'm quick to say:

Lord, forgive me.
Forgive me of my pride.
Forgive me for thinking I'm invincible.
Forgive me for ever thinking that I am you.
At times I'm an idiot. I need you, Lord.

Recently I had a week in which my goal was "just to make it through it." I knew it was going to be a tough week before it even began. And so Monday morning, I jumped in headfirst, wading through e-mails, meetings, hard conversations, and deadlines. Just hours into the week, I was already tired. Too busy to breathe. Too busy to think straight. Too busy to talk with God. I just kept going. *I just need to make it through,* I reminded myself.

The rest of the week was no different. Watching me during that week would have been like watching a bad car accident in slow motion. Tuesday came and went. Then it was Hump Day. I was halfway there. Thursday came and went. By Friday I was a crazy man—stressed, exhausted, with zero patience. I came home only to be greeted by four kids who were excited to see their dad. I said hello and made it to my bedroom as quickly as I could. I closed the door behind me so they couldn't bother me. I had nothing to offer my kids or anyone else. I ate by myself and was relieved once the kids went to bed. Thank goodness I don't have to see them anymore. Horrible to admit, but it's how I felt.

That night I went on my walk.[13] Even though the weekend had arrived, all I could think about was work. My mind was racing, trying to think of what I had most likely missed. I sent e-mails to myself as I walked. I made a call to a coworker. I was still wound so tight and even more tired than I had been before I left the office just hours earlier. I was done.

I was walking on autopilot. I honestly don't remember which path I took. I was like a zombie from *The Walking Dead*. Blocks away from home, my body stopped moving. In the middle of the sidewalk, I froze. I had come to the end of myself. And the words finally came out:

Lord, I need your help.

These were the words that I should have uttered first thing Monday morning.

These were words that I could have spoken at any point throughout the week.

So why did I wait until I was completely exhausted before I reached out my hand to God?

Why do we wait to cry out? Why are we so slow to learn? Why do we pride-fully think we can make it through life, or even a week, on our own?

Lord, forgive us.

———

"Come to me.... And you will find rest."

Jesus invites us daily. It's not a onetime thing or a limited opportunity. The invitation is always there. Whenever we're tired. Or burnt out. Whenever we're exhausted. And even when we're not. He always invites us.

"Come."

"You will find rest for your souls."

All we need to do is pray, to talk with God.

All we need to do is say the words:

Lord, I need you.

12

You need an anchor.

Sailors throw their anchors downwards;
we throw ours upwards.

—Charles Spurgeon

A few summers ago, I decided to save up my money for something big. My family and I love to go to the lake[1], so we decided it was time to make the big purchase, if you know what I'm saying. We couldn't wait to fish away from shore. We wanted to cruise the lake in style. It took some time to save, since money doesn't grow on trees. But we finally came up with the cash to purchase the big, the beautiful, Wave Dolphin paddleboat.

I don't want to brag, but yes, this baby is a five-seater, and it's fully equipped with cup holders and a canopy that is virtually useless.[2]

So we bought this four-hundred-dollar "boat" and were excited to get it out on the lake. I piled all the kids in, and even though there were some fairly good waves, I wasn't too concerned. It's a Wave Dolphin, after all. Pretty much the Mercedes of paddleboats. And it came from Tractor Supply, where most people buy their boats, right?[3] I was pumped!

We pushed out from shore, and I started pedaling—only to realize several things. First, I was completely out of shape. That's putting it nicely. Second, the waves were bigger than I thought. The wind likes to blow here in South Dakota. A lot. And third, this wasn't a boat; it was more of a treadmill. Like a full-body exercise machine.

We made our way a fair distance from shore, and after five minutes, I decided it was time to head back. That's when I realized that I couldn't turn. You know the little turn-steering thing? It would turn one direction but not the other. So I start pedaling as hard as I could, only to go in circles. Meanwhile, we were drifting farther and farther out onto the lake, pushed by the waves. Not good! Lake Albert isn't a small lake.[4]

My oldest started noticing that I was getting stressed. I'm not sure why. Maybe it was the crazy look on my face. Or the fact that I was about to pass out from the intense cardio workout, something I hadn't done for years. Or ever. He asked if everything was okay. Then my daughter started freaking out. Internally, I was freaking out as well.

The kids started crying. My son Wilson had his arms wrapped completely around my neck, squeezing as hard as he could. Even without him choking me, I was already concerned about getting enough oxygen to my brain. My legs were burning from pedaling. And for maybe the first time in my life, I didn't have my cell phone with me. Seriously?

It was an awesome, epic-fail moment as a dad.

Dear God, please get me to shore!
Lord, why have you forsaken me?
I promise I'll start working out! Deliver me, Jesus!
Even though this lake is only eight feet deep, am I going to
die, Lord—from a heart attack?

The whole time we were going in circles, drifting farther and farther out on the lake, all I could think was that this was supposed to be so much fun. In this moment, I just wished I had an anchor.

If I had an anchor, at least we wouldn't drift out even farther. I could catch my breath for a second. Or we could just stay right where we were. The Wave Dolphins come equipped with cup holders and a canopy, but no anchors.

I so badly needed an anchor.

———

Now, I'd like to think that I'm a fairly stable person, that I have a level head on my shoulders—whatever that means—and that I have my life, priorities, career, and relationship with Jesus all figured out.

I'd like to think that I'm kind of staying in my lane in life. Doing my thing. Consistently doing the right things and making the right choices. I'd like to think I'm unmoved by the stuff that comes my way. Completely confident in who I am. I am a grown adult, after all.

I'd like to think, and have others believe, that my life is great. It's fun and carefree and perfect. No worries. You've seen my pictures on Facebook, right? My kids are always smiling. The house is always clean. My work and marriage have never been better.

But the truth is, on any given day, it feels a bit like I'm stuck on a crappy paddleboat. A paddleboat that just goes round and round in circles. I feel like I'm constantly changing, one moment to the next.

One moment I'm worrying about my kids, and the next, I'm worrying about something I said.

One moment I'm full of pride and think I've arrived, and the next, I feel crazy insecure and wonder if any good can happen through me.

One moment I'm not struggling with temptation, and the next, I find temptation everywhere and struggle with the same crap I've dealt with for years.

One moment I feel like a great dad and a good friend and love comes easily, and the next, my kids drive me crazy and I struggle to show my love for them or anyone else.

One moment I feel like I have my priorities figured out and my work and home life are balanced, and the next, it feels like I'm failing at life.

Internally, I'm constantly changing. And it doesn't help that there is so much in life over which we have zero control. That's hard for a control freak like me. You too?

Think about it: We have very little control over the things other people say and do to us, yet their words and actions can impact us so much. No matter how hard we try, we can't control our kids, our parents, our spouse, our classmates, or our insane coworkers and the choices they make. I don't know about you, but I've certainly tried—and failed—to control them. Honestly, I can't imagine how much time and energy I use trying to control every aspect of my life and everyone else's.

As with life, so it is with each day. Everything is constantly changing, whether I want it to or not. As a result, it sometimes feels like I'm going in circles. It seems like I'm pedaling as fast as I possibly can yet not going in any specific direction. Within my soul, it feels like I'm constantly changing. From one moment to the next.

———

Throughout the Bible we see a variety of different titles and descriptions for Jesus. We hear him called everything from our Savior, to the Bread of Life, to the Vine. He's the King of kings and the Lord of lords. We could go on and on.

One of the books in the New Testament, Hebrews, is a letter written to a group of Christians. No one's really quite sure who wrote the letter, but at one point, the author describes Jesus and the hope found in Jesus. It tells us that *Jesus is a strong and trustworthy anchor for our souls.*[5]

This means that Jesus and the hope found in Jesus brings us stability and security. He's an anchor!

At the time Hebrews was written, an anchor was often used as a metaphor for something being unmovable. This means that our souls, the deepest part of who we are, can become steady and secure if we do one thing: we hold on to Jesus. If rely on Jesus and talk with him, then our souls are tied to something greater than ourselves. And we become anchored. Unmovable.

When it comes to worry, instead of riding the waves of anxiety, we trust in our anchor, Jesus, who is all-powerful and good and holds us steady.

When it comes to insecurity, instead of being tossed back and forth by shifting winds, we are steadied in Jesus.

When it comes to pride, Jesus keeps us on our knees. And when we're on our knees, Jesus gives us the strength to stand. Reminding us that only he can navigate the waters of our lives.

When it comes to temptation, instead of being swayed by the lure of instant gratification that will only leave us broken, Jesus, our anchor, gives us steady self-control.

When it comes to self-worth, instead of relying on our feelings, thoughts, and the ever-changing opinions of other people, we have constant assurance of our value from Jesus—our anchor.

We have no reason to pedal in circles on the lake, going nowhere except farther from shore. We don't have to drift aimlessly out to sea. Jesus is a strong and trustworthy anchor for our souls. He keeps us where we need to be.

———

At some point during that unforgettable day on the lake, I discovered that in order to turn the paddleboat, I needed to make sure the weight was distributed evenly. *Can it really be this simple?* So I scooted to the center of the boat, straddled the steering thingy, and pedaled like crazy! Did I mention that I'm out of shape?

I pedaled hard for a while, then stopped to rest. I pedaled hard again, and then stopped. At one point, I considered jumping out and pulling the boat to shore, but I worried that would make the kids freak out even more—if such a thing were possible. They were already going nuts.

I finally got us to the shore, and when I did I immediately fell to the ground. I collapsed. I was stressed, overwhelmed, exhausted, and just done. My kids got out of the Wave Dolphin, walked up to me and just stood there. Silent. Wiping their tears away. They just stared at me. They were probably thinking, *Is he dead or something?* I hope I didn't scar them for life.

Are you tired of going in circles—being consumed by worry, constantly wondering about your worth, changing one moment to the next? I know I am.

Here's good news: Jesus is a strong and trustworthy anchor for our souls.

When we feel like we're on a paddleboat in the middle of an ocean, we can hold on to Jesus and claim him as our anchor. At any point, we can pray. At any point, we can talk to God.

Lord Jesus, today I want to be tied to something
*   greater than myself.*
Instead of basing my life on my feelings,
Or the thoughts of others,
Or what I think,
Or my circumstances . . .
I want to base my life on you, Father.

I want to find my security and my strength in you.
I want my soul, all that I am, to be tied to and anchored
  to only you.

As with other things, this anchoring in Jesus isn't a onetime rescue. Instead it's something we need to claim daily, some days more than others. When we claim Jesus as our anchor, we surrender ourselves to him.

Jesus is the strong and trustworthy anchor for our souls.

———

A few months back, I got the chance to attend one of my favorite conferences. Some of the greatest leaders in the world were going to be there, and I knew it was going to be awesome. I couldn't wait!

But as soon as I got there, I became overwhelmed with insecurity. Now I've struggled with insecurity ever since elementary school.[6] As a kid, I wanted to fit in more than anything else. I would have done anything to be cool. Looking back at my pictures from fourth grade, it's clear to me now why I wasn't. Even though I wore cool Hypercolor shirts, I was as awkward and nerdy as can be. I tried everything to fit in. I tried to talk like other kids. Tried to act like someone else. I wanted so desperately to belong. Each day I felt like I was pedaling and pedaling and pedaling, just trying to survive.

Later on, even as a "cool kid" in high school, I worried that people would figure out that I wasn't anything special. Even now I'm thirty-five years old, a husband, a dad, "successful" at what I do, and in many ways things haven't changed. I'm still unsure of my worth and identity. I'm still human. And like most humans, one of my great desires is to fit in and be important in the eyes of someone else.

As soon as I arrived at the conference that day, I immediately began comparing myself to others.

These are some of the greatest leaders in the world. They're pastoring churches ten times bigger than mine, I thought. *Why am I here? I'm just some random nobody from South Dakota. They probably don't even know where South Dakota is.*

I became restless, second-guessing every word I said. I walked around aimlessly and tried to act like someone I wasn't, tried to make myself look better than I was. By the end of the day, I was totally drained. I was on a paddleboat again, pedaling and pedaling and pedaling.

The conference should have been awesome, yet I was miserable. When I got back to my hotel room on the second night, I finally stopped. I got on my knees and began to talk with God. The words just came out:

> *Lord, I'm tired and my soul is seasick from being all over*
> *the place.*
> *Father, I'm terrible at trying to be someone I'm not.*
> *Jesus, help me to cling to you.*
> *Help me to find my unchanging worth in you.*
> *Father, I'm best at being the person you created me to be.*
> *Jesus, please come and be my anchor.*

In that moment, peace fell over me. The whole time, I had been pedaling around for no reason. How God viewed me hadn't changed. At no point was my worth or value in question. My anchor, Jesus, hadn't moved. He was strong and secure. I just wasn't holding on to him.

The next day I grabbed lunch with a close friend, who was speaking at the conference. I shared with him everything I had been struggling with and my prayers from the night before. He quickly assured me that he, and everyone else, were no different. He was struggling himself with many of the same exact feelings. Without God, we're all adrift, battling against the current. It's exhausting. It's only because of God's grace, his anchor, that we're stable.

In case you didn't hear it, Jesus is the strong and trustworthy anchor for our souls.

At any point, we can talk with him and hold on to him.

At any point, we can cling and strap ourselves to him.

At any point, he will steady us.

13

You want to be used by God.

I am no longer my own, but thine.

—John Wesley

I grew up in a home filled with music. My mom started playing piano when she was three years old and played weekly in church starting in seventh grade.[1] Even after having kids of her own, she taught piano lessons out of our home. With her first-year students, the music wasn't always pretty, but it often filled our home.

I loved to sing with my mom. She'd play the piano as I sat alongside her on the wooden bench and sang. "How Great Thou Art." "In the Garden." "Because He Lives." We'd flip through the old Lutheran hymnal until we found a song we both liked, and then Mom would play.

My favorite song to sing with her was "Here I Am, Lord"[2]:

Who will bear My light to them? . . .
I will go, Lord, if You lead me.

I didn't understand the words I was singing. But early on, this song was planted within me. It was a song I would cross paths with again.

———

As I've mentioned earlier, one of my greatest struggles in life has been and continues to be the feeling of being completely inadequate. Whether it was playing football at recess during the fourth grade[3] or speaking in front of my communications class in college, I felt inadequate and unsure in every situation. Even in my adult years, I have felt disqualified from being used to do anything important, particularly by God.

I've always been quite average. I was good enough at football that I wasn't picked last during recess, but I was too short and slow to be a great athlete. I made the honor roll in high school but was never at the top of the class. And although I laboriously prepared solid speeches for my communications class, I always seemed to mumble the words during the delivery. In my appearance, gifts, skills, and expertise, I've always been average. Everything I could do, someone else could do much better.

When you feel ordinary, average, or less skilled, it's always easier to play things safe, isn't it? To blend in. Don't raise your hand. Don't step out. Take no chances. Don't try to be used by God. To be honest, "safe" is where I wanted to stay. Why risk failing if you don't have to? Why take the chance of looking stupid if it's not required? As a young person, I didn't mind staying right where I was.

In the Bible, we see all kinds of ordinary people being used by God. Some of them were actually below average in some ways. Abraham was too old. Moses stuttered. David had a moral failure. Lazarus was dead! Their stories are powerful accounts of God using average people for great things. But I still struggled to connect with them. Yes, they appeared to be quite average, but how average could they be if they're mentioned in the Bible? I know *I'm* not mentioned in the Bible.

———

Some years passed by, and on one of my visits home from college, my mom pulled out the hymnal and we sang "Here I Am, Lord" again.

Who will bear My light to them? Whom shall I send?

This time around, the words took on a completely different meaning. I thought of my first conversation with God out under the stars. I thought of how God had brought light into my darkness, how knowing Jesus had changed everything about me.

Whom shall I send?

My answer: someone else.

I wanted to be used by God, but what could he do through me? I wanted to "bear his light," but I figured I'd probably cause more harm than good. My anxiety level rose just thinking about it. As I sat on that piano bench, a tug-of-war took place within me. I longed to tell the whole world what God had done in my life. But I figured it was probably best for me to stay out of the way so a more qualified person could do so. I felt God speaking to me, but I once again felt inadequate in every way—disqualified to be used, particularly by him.

As we sang on, however, I heard my soul speak the words:

I will go, Lord, if You lead me.

I still didn't fully understand what the words meant, and I still felt 100 percent sure God couldn't use me. But a small part of me was willing to say yes. Something within me couldn't say no any longer.

Over the following weeks and months, I kept hearing myself quietly speak the words, "Here I am, Lord." *If you lead, I'll follow. Then it's on you, right?*

———

Within each of us, there's a desire to be used by God. We want to take part in something great, to make a difference for good. We want our lives to matter. Ask a person, "What would you do if you knew you couldn't fail?" and long-kept dreams will flow out. The person will seem to come alive right before your eyes. It's almost like the person begins to glow. Whether it's a sixty-five-year-old retiree, a young stay-at-home mom, or a seemingly successful person at the top of his career, the story is always the same. When I meet someone for coffee, I'm likely to hear a secret aspiration pour out:

"I've always wanted to be a teacher. A doctor. A police officer."

"I've always wanted to write a book."

"My whole life, I've wanted to make a difference in the lives of others."

"I have this desire to help people. I want my life to matter."

When we think of "great things," we typically picture a story that will make the news or get shared in a book. But I'm beginning to realize that with God, anything can be a big thing. In the Bible, we see that through an act as simple as opening up our homes for guests, we might be entertaining angels. Just offering a person a glass of water is really an act of kindness toward Jesus himself. Sometimes the smallest things make the biggest difference.[4]

Looking back at my life, I'm amazed by how God continually prepares us for the question "Whom shall I send?"

When I was a kid, my mom and I volunteered at a local nursing home each Wednesday. She played the music and we both sang for the folks living there.[5] At first I was terrified by the "old people." They were excited to see me, but I was scared to death to see them. They all wanted to squeeze my cheeks and shake my hand. I didn't want to be there. But as the people slowly wheeled their chairs into the room, Mom would begin playing the piano as I handed out the songbooks. Before long, I loved helping people find the right page so they could sing along.

I also didn't like hospitals or funeral homes. They were depressing and smelled weird. As I walked past a hospital room, I always worried about what I'd see as I peeked in. During college, I heard about a flower shop that needed a delivery boy. I needed money during the summer, and I figured it couldn't be that hard to deliver flowers. I had no idea that most of a flower shop's deliveries go to hospitals and funeral homes. Many of the flowers sent to hospital rooms were ordered by loved ones who couldn't be there in person. Before long, instead of dropping off the flowers and leaving, I often asked the patients how they were doing and mentioned that I would be praying for them. Sometimes I commented on how pretty their flowers were. Even though this was a small, simple gesture, I left feeling that I had made a difference in people's day.

Who would have known that years later I would take a job that would require me to be comfortable in nursing homes, hospitals, and funeral homes?

With God, all things are big things. He's constantly at work, shaping and preparing us for the next adventure that will take us to the places we least expect.

———

A few more years would pass before I sang "Here I Am, Lord" again. The next time was in Bismarck, North Dakota. I had finished seminary and was being ordained. The ordination service in the Methodist Church is a formal, traditional service.[6] That year it was held in a beautiful old Methodist church.[7] The church had tall stained glass windows and a large organ with pipes. The sanctuary was filled with people. At the very end of the ordination service, of all songs, we sang:

Who will bear My light to them? . . .
I will go, Lord, if You lead me.

I was overwhelmed by God's faithfulness. For years he had been speaking to me. Preparing me. Directing me. He wanted to use *me.*

The truth is that, on our own, we *are* in inadequate. In every way. On our own, we are disqualified from being used by God.

Thankfully, it's not about who we are. It's only about who God is. It's about his gifts. His abilities. His strength. His wisdom. And his potential. Not ours.

Oddly enough, the only time we can't be used by God is when we think we *are* adequate.

Again, it's about God, not us. It's about trusting him more than we trust ourselves. God only requires us to be willing, to simply say, "Here I am, Lord." Not once or a few times in life, but daily.

> *Lord, I'm scared. But here I am.*
> *Father, this doesn't make sense. But here I am.*
> *I feel foolish. I feel half-sick. But here I am.*
> *This seems so awkward. But here I am.*
> *Lord, I want my day to matter. I want to be used by you.*
>   *Here I am.*

———

One of the clearest ways I can see that someone is growing in his or her relationship with God is the person's willingness to say yes to God. To big things. To small things. And particularly to things that don't make sense or are out of one's comfort zone.

I think of a friend who went part-time at his six-figure banking job so he could start a side business that he had dreamed and prayed about for years.

I also think of one of my best friends who became a real-estate agent right out of college.[8] He was good at it and quickly became one of the top agents in Sioux Falls, which was awesome, but he always felt a tug to go to seminary. Everyone, including me, thought he was crazy, but nothing was cooler than the day he called and said, "I just applied to seminary, and I'm wondering if you'd be a reference for me."

And then there's the lady who, after trying to get pregnant for years, conceived, only to have a miscarriage. Broken and upset with God, she ended up at church "of all places," as she put it. God began to heal her. When I asked her if she might be willing to share her story with the church, she said yes. She encouraged countless women and couples who had experienced the same thing themselves.

Whether it's seeing a need and filling it,

Or raising a hand,

Helping someone,

Applying for a job,

Making a phone call,

Telling someone about Jesus,

Moving forward with the project,

Be willing to say . . .

"Here I am, Lord."

The longer I follow the Lord, the more often I find myself speaking those words throughout each day. I want to be used by him. But at the same time, I've never felt more inadequate than I do today.

Am I still able to be used by God? The church I pastor has grown from thirty-two people to thousands. Am I still able? I know the truth: I'm still the same average person I've always been, but with less hair. I still get nervous before I preach. I still get uneasy before making a decision. At times I'm paralyzed by fear and self-doubt. At times I'm tempted to walk away from it all. I'm afraid that people will realize just how average I am.

God, can you still use me? Am I adequate and able to do this?

The truth is, *I've* never been adequate. It's been God the whole time.[9] So there's nothing different in what lies ahead. On my own, I am completely inadequate. If you need proof that God can use you, look no further. I'm your guy.

Feel inadequate? Lacking? Insufficient? Disqualified to be used?

We're right where we need to be in order to be used by God. All we have to do is say yes.

When we start saying yes to him, he'll begin to do the impossible in and through us. Things that blow us away. Things that we could never ever imagine. Things that will leave us completely speechless.

When we're willing to say yes to the small things, he'll give us opportunities to say yes to big things. This is the story of my life.

Adam, will you follow me?

Yes.

Share your story at church as a junior in high school?

Yes.

Go to seminary even though you have a business degree?

Yes.

Start a church even though you think it's a crazy idea?

Yes.

Launch a second campus. And then a third, fourth, and fifth?

Yes.

Even though you're not a writer and you have zero qualifications to write a book, write one?

Ummm . . . Yes, Lord.[10]

The best part is that when God does the impossible through average people, we clearly know it's all God. It's because of his abilities and not ours. Only he gets the credit. Only he gets the glory.

"Who will bear My light to them?" Jesus still asks. Our simple prayer:

Here I am, Lord.

14

You're trying to extend grace.

Grace defies reason and logic.

—Bono

When I hear the word *grace,* different things come to mind.

I think about the hymn: "Amazing grace, how sweet the sound, that saved a wretch like me." As a kid, I found this song confusing. I thought it used the word *wrench. Is God a mechanic or something?*

I think about the scene in the classic movie *Christmas Vacation,* where Aunt Bethany is asked to say grace.[1] She responds with, "Grace? She passed away thirty years ago!"[2]

I also think about the sweet old lady named Grace whose lawn I used to mow when I was a teenager. She always offered me lemonade, and she paid well![3]

The word might bring different things to mind. And it's possible you've heard this churchy word a lot.

But what does grace actually mean?

Put simply, grace is being given something that we don't deserve.

It's being given something that we didn't earn. Something that we're not entitled to. Something we don't and shouldn't expect. It's an unmerited gift.

And grace comes in many forms.

Grace is receiving kindness after being rude to a person.

Grace is looking for the good in someone—a neighbor, a sibling, a spouse—instead of seeing the person's obvious faults.

Grace is going out of our way for a complete stranger.

Grace is being given a second chance—and then possibly a third and fourth chance.

Grace is being willing to help someone, to listen to someone who has nothing to offer in return.

Grace is telling a close friend the hard truth when no one else is willing to.

Grace is extending forgiveness. It's being faithful. It's being patient with someone who absolutely has not earned it.

Grace is loving someone who's hard to love.

At the basis of a deep friendship, great workplace, good marriage, or solid family, you will find grace.

And as human beings, we long for grace, don't we? It moves us to tears when we see it in a viral video or in the life of another person.

Grace is a beautiful thing that touches us at our core.

And yet the conversation completely changes when it comes to extending grace to others. Offering grace to others is challenging. It's hard. It's anything but easy. Why? Because the other person doesn't deserve it! And when we've been hurt by someone, we want justice, right?

I mean, if you only knew my brother, my aunt, my ex, my neighbor.

If you had been there, then you'd understand.

If you could see how hard my spouse, my child, my boss is to live with.

If you saw how busy my schedule is.

If you only knew the whole story.

Grace is so hard to give because the other person doesn't deserve it. And yet that's exactly what grace is. It's undeserved.

Throughout the New Testament, we see grace. "It is by grace you have been saved,"[4] Paul wrote. Jesus is "full of grace and truth."[5]

I know for myself that when I hear about grace, I typically think of receiving it. Yet listen to these words written by Paul.

"You've heard, of course, about the responsibility to distribute God's grace."[6]

Paul is basically saying: "I know this is really obvious, and I know you've probably heard it a bunch of times, but just to share it again, as followers of Jesus, we are responsible for distributing God's grace."

He's saying, as followers of Jesus we are responsible for showing and extending grace to others. It's not optional. We don't get to pick and choose when we want to and for whom. It does not depend on the other person and whether he deserves it or not. Paul tells us that we are *responsible* for sharing and distributing God's grace with *everyone*.

Now maybe I'm shallow, but I just have to ask: Why should we? I mean, why should we offer grace to others? Why are *we* responsible for distributing it? And do we *have* to?

As a general rule, human beings don't deserve grace, and to add insult to injury, they are often ungrateful when they are shown grace. And they're hard to love. And they're wishy-washy. And they're selfish and arrogant and nasty and cranky and everything in between.

The last thing that comes to my mind is offering grace to people like that.

But in one sentence, Paul explains why we should give grace.

"I became a servant of the gospel," Paul says.

In other words, he became a distributor of God's grace. Why? "Because of the grace that God showed" him.[7]

Why should we extend grace? Paul says, simply because of the grace God has shown and given to me. The grace that God has shown and given to you. The grace that he's shown and given to us.

I am the ambassador of the grace that God first extended to me.

It's the same reason that we're able to love. "We love because God first loved us."[8] It's the same reason we're able to forgive. "As the Lord forgave you, so also forgive each other."[9]

We offer God's grace to others, and are able to do so, because of the amazing and unending grace that God has shown us.

We've received it. Now we must give it.

———

For me, just thinking about the grace that God has shown me is completely overwhelming. Knowing my own faults, my shortcomings, and my mistakes, big and small, puts me in awe of God's grace toward me. I'm such a slow learner. I'm so quick to be self-centered. I'm quick to want to do things my way. And yet I see his grace in the patience he has with me. I see his grace in the fact that he loves me, and that he loves deeply enough to tell me the hard truth. I see his grace in all that he's given me and all that he's provided for me.

My life is far from perfect, yet when I look at what God has done in my life, all I can say is *Lord, I don't deserve this.*

Once more, though, that's exactly what grace is all about. And when we begin to understand even a hint of the grace that God has given to us, something changes. Our immediate question changes. It changes from "Why should we extend grace to others?" to "How can we not do so?"

God has covered us with so much grace, how could we not extend it to the people in our lives?

Lord, on my own I have no grace. Please help me to offer yours.

Jesus, help me to extend grace to the people in my life.

Lord, help me to realize the amazing grace that you've given me.

Father, how can I not be patient and kind with my coworker when you've been so patient and kind with me?

Jesus, help me to forgive, show kindness, and have understanding toward my ex.

Lord, help me to distribute your grace.

It's true—we should forgive freely and simply because of the grace that God has given us. Still, there are times when grace is incredibly difficult to distribute. At times it's grueling, particularly when we've been hurt on a deeper level. Times when physically or emotionally we've been impacted in a way that changes the rest of our life.

At times like this, it's *only* by talking with God. It's only through prayer and staying connected with God that we're able to extend grace to others.

Recently, my friend Justin shared a part of his story with me. His dad was a successful banker and his mom stayed at home with the kids. In order to get his career off the ground, his father had to work long and late hours—to the point where it began to seem that there was more to the story. There were times his dad was supposedly working, but he wasn't at the bank. This became the norm until one day his dad came home and announced he was having an affair with his assistant and wanted a divorce.

Justin can remember sitting in the stairway with his little brother, listening to his parents argue in the living room. Justin was only five at the time. The argument came to an end. His dad left the house, and his mom came into the boys' room. She did her best to explain what was happening and what would change. She said, "From here on out, we're going to be on our own and we have to rely on God." That night, at the age of five, my friend invited Jesus into his life.

Justin, his mom, and his brother later moved to a different state. His mom finished school and got a job. "I was only a kid," Justin told me, "so I didn't fully understand. But I hurt for my mom. She was a complete mess."

Meanwhile, Justin's dad stayed back in the same town and continued both his career and his relationship with his assistant. He eventually married her. Throughout elementary school, my friend and his brother would see their dad one weekend a month. But as the years passed, the visits with his father became fewer and more sporadic. They often went months without seeing each other. Justin's dad consistently chose work, his wife, and his new life over his kids.

Years later, when Justin and his brother were in high school, their dad called and said their broken relationship was all their fault. When in reality, it was all clearly *his* fault.

"My little brother was so angry, and so was I," Justin told me. "On top of all that, I was still hurting for my mom. I didn't want to talk with my dad. I didn't want to see him. I didn't want anything to do with him. There was no relationship left. I was done."

Justin went to college, and one day his dad reached out by e-mail. He had switched careers. And to no one's surprise, the marriage with his former assistant had ended in divorce.

"Looking back, I know now that God was at work within me," Justin said. "He was softening my heart toward my dad. God helped me to see my dad differently. I was still angry. I hated what he did to my mom, but I still wanted a relationship with him."

"My dad wanted a relationship with me as well."

Justin's dad asked if he would be willing to go on a trip together. Seeing the effort, Justin said yes to the trip. He also began to pray for his dad and his feelings toward his dad.

"On so many levels, it was healing. For my dad. For me."

Now that he has kids of his own, it's amazing to see grace at work in my friend's life. In his entire family. His dad, now known as Grandpa, is fully in the picture. My friend has a dad again. And his kids have a grandpa who is crazy in love with them.

Even still, for Justin, extending grace has been a process.

"I never thought I would have the strength to forgive my dad. I didn't think I could show him grace and love after all the hurt and pain he caused our family. I had to spend time with God, read the Bible, and talk with God. For years I wanted to be angry, but the more I talked with God, the more I realized that I couldn't. I came to see that just as God extended grace to me, I needed to extend it to my dad.

"Even today I need to continue talking with God for grace to be present toward my father."

———

Extending God's grace to someone when we've been hurt at the core is impossible on our own. It's something that can happen only by being supernaturally connected to God.

It's only possible as a result of praying.

It comes through long and hard conversations with God, by talking with him in the morning, throughout the day, each week, and maybe on an anniversary of a difficult event. Fully trusting, relying on, and talking with God.

Prayer empowers us to extend grace to the person who has hurt us more than anyone else on the planet.

> God, I give this person over to you again today.
> I'm still hurting. Help me to extend grace.
> Jesus, I thought I was past the anger. Past the bitterness.
>   Past these feelings.
> I need your grace because I have none to give.

When I read Paul's description of grace and his challenge to "distribute" God's grace, all I can think of is an overwhelming amount of grace. I'm not talking about just a little bit of grace, or kinda sorta giving grace, or handing it out to a few people like it's a cute project.

Instead, I picture us handing out mass quantities of grace to everyone. I picture crates and crates stacked with bottles and bottles of grace, God's grace.

Grace that doesn't come from us, but only from God. And because this grace is from God, there's an endless supply. It's the same grace that we've been showered with ourselves. And now we get to hand it out.

We get to generously distribute it to the people around us, one person at a time, starting with those who are closest to us.

We get to hand out grace through our words. Words that give life to our spouse. Words that give life to our coworkers. Words that give life to our kids, our siblings, our family members who drive us crazy, our ex or someone who has hurt us in the past. Words that give life to the waitress who is serving us. Words that give life to the people we disagree with.

I picture us being quick to say, "Thank you." Quick to say, "I'm sorry." Quick to say, "Great job." Quick to say, "I love you."

I picture a grace big enough to remove gossip, jealousy, and negativity from our mouths and our hearts.

I think about all of us handing out grace through our actions as well.

I picture us serving the person in front of us, regardless of who that person is, and extending kindness to the grumpy people in our lives.[10]

I envision us going out of our way to help a person in need, a friend, or a complete stranger. Acknowledging the person in the room who is lowest on the totem pole and treating him like he's at the top.

I imagine us looking for opportunities to give away our time and money. And not doing so sparingly but generously. I see us remaining faithful to a person even when she hasn't been faithful to us.

I see us being quick to forgive.

Just to be clear, showing grace to a person doesn't mean that we condone that person's actions. It's not about being a pushover. It's not signing off on someone's mistreatment of us and saying it's okay. It's not allowing others to walk all over us. Sometimes the most gracious thing one person can do for another is tell her that what she's doing isn't okay and that she needs help.

Through both our words and our actions, I picture handing out mass quantities of grace to person after person after person. Distributing God's grace, not our own, to every last person we come in contact with.

And how is this possible? By talking with the One who first extended grace to us.

Grace is an undeserved gift. We have received it. Now it's ours to give.

ONLY THE
BEGINNING

15

Capture the moment.

He walks with me, and he talks with me.

—Charles Austin Miles

I love making moments. Watching my youngest son learn how to walk. Going on vacation with my family. Taking my beautiful wife out on a date.

Again, I love making moments and, of course, I have perfect pictures from all of these moments too. How could I not, armed 24/7 with my cellular camera, I mean, my cell phone. Always ready to take a picture and post it on Instagram. It's bizarre how easily we're able to share our moments with the world at the click of a button.

But lately, scrolling back through all of my photos, I've been wondering, *Did I actually experience any of these moments?*

I have the pictures. Pictures I can show and talk about with others—even years later. But did I actually experience the moments themselves? I mean, did I delight in seeing my son walk for the first time, celebrating with him? Did I soak up every moment of time away with my family on vacation? Did I enjoy the time spent talking to and being with my wife?

Or did I just take a few pictures so that I could talk about later? Did I do it only so I can appear to have my life all together? So I can brag about my experiences?

I wonder something similar about my time with God.

I think a lot *about* God. But how often do I actually *experience* him? I talk a lot *about* him, but how often do I actually talk *with* him?

In general, Christians seem to talk a lot about God, don't we? Which isn't inherently a bad thing. We talk about him with friends, with coworkers, with complete strangers. We write things about him online. Our bumper stickers talk about him. We regularly discuss God in church and in small groups. Sometimes even our cheesy T-shirts talk about him.

Once more, this isn't necessarily a bad thing. But again, how often do we actually talk *with* him?

As a pastor, it's my job to talk about God. I get paid to share insights about him, to preach on what the Bible says about him. I post on Twitter about him. Sometimes Facebook. But sometimes it feels like I've talked *about* God all day without spending a single moment talking *with* God. Truth be told, it's easy to go for days or weeks at a time without saying a single word to God.

———

One of the things that seems to trip people up when it comes to prayer is a lack of knowledge about God.

"I'm new to God and church and everything."

"I don't know much about God and the Bible."

"Even though I grew up in the church, there's so much I just don't know."

Because we feel like we don't know much about God, we believe the lie that we can't talk with him. We assume that we first have to read more, learn more, and know more about him. We think we need to become "good enough" to talk with God, but nothing could be further from the truth. It's not about gaining knowledge.

Jesus was often at odds with those who claimed to know everything about God. The people who claimed to have God all figured out (and were proud of their knowledge) were the ones who Jesus often called out as hypocrites.

Yes, it's important to learn more about God. Yes, it's important to spend time reading the Bible, learning more about who God is. But nothing can replace simply being with God. The truth is, there is a big difference between going to church and truly experiencing God. And we come to know God best through firsthand experience, by actually talking with him.

————

The summer before my senior year of college, through the most unusual circumstances, I found myself filling in for a pastor in Wahpeton, North

Dakota.[1] The pastor was taking a few months off, and the church let me fill the gap. It turned out that the pastor had a daughter my age. And well, she was beautiful. But for the first half of the summer, she was in France.

Because I was a young single guy, every lady in the church wanted to set me up with this girl. They talked relentlessly about Becky Spahr. I would visit an older lady who was homebound, share a few Bible verses, ask how she was doing, and before I'd leave, she'd ask if I knew Becky Spahr. "She's so nice. She's the same age as you. You need to meet her."[2]

I'd stop by the hospital to pray for a lady who had cancer. We'd talk and pray, and before leaving I'd hear, "You and Becky Spahr need to meet sometime. She loves the Lord. She's in her last year of college too. You should go on a date with her."

After church, I'd be shaking hands with people as they left, and someone would say, "You and Becky Spahr would be perfect together."

For a couple of months, I heard all kinds of things about Becky Spahr. It was almost strange how much I knew about her. But although I knew a lot about her, I didn't actually know her. At all. I felt a bit like a stalker. She sounded great, but I knew that at some point, I would actually have to meet her and talk with her in order to really know her.

Once Becky returned home from France, I gathered the courage to call her. We went on a walk. She talked about her summer up to that point, and I shared about mine. We talked as we walked. Now I wasn't just learning about her. I was getting to know her, and I wanted to know more.

———

I wonder how many of us will spend most of our lives talking about God instead of talking with him. More personally, will I spend most of my life only talking about God?

Will *you* spend most of your life solely talking *about* God?

I mean, will you be satisfied to know him mostly from afar? Collecting mere facts about him and "pictures" of him? Or will you spend your life fully experiencing him? Enjoying him. Delighting in him. Soaking up each and every moment with him. Getting to know him by talking with him.

The apostle Paul wrote a letter to a group of Christians in Philippi, and he boldly declared, "I want to know Christ."[3]

No biggie, right? Paul wanted to know Jesus. Who doesn't? This word *know,* however, means something more than we normally think.[4] In Jewish culture, this same word was often used to describe boomshakalaka.[5]

Not clear enough? Sex!

Now obviously, Paul wasn't saying that he wanted anything physical with God. Instead he was saying that he wanted to know God at the deepest, most intimate level possible. He didn't just want to know about him. He wanted to know him personally, fully, and intimately. Paul wanted to know Christ's heart. Every part of who God is.

Paul knew that our hearts are created for intimacy with God. We have a longing within us to know him. We were designed for a relationship with God, one that will grow deeper for all of eternity. To talk with God all the days of our lives.

My mom and dad have been married for forty years now. Sometimes Mom will say, "Even after all these years, I'm still coming to learn new things about your dad. The longer I'm with him, the more I know and love him."

When it comes to God, my soul feels the same way about him. I've been following Jesus for seventeen years now. And the longer I follow God, the more I want to know him.

> *Father, I've experienced your peace, but I want to know it more fully.*
> *I've been changed by your love, but I want to know it more deeply.*
> *I know you, God, but I feel like I haven't even scratched the surface.*
> *Lord, I want to be with you. I want to experience more of you. I want to talk with you.*

———

Over that summer in Wahpeton, Becky and I hung out a few more times with groups of friends, but I concluded there was no hope. Not a chance that she'd be interested in this guy. The summer came to a close, and I was done filling in for the pastor. My mom came the last Sunday I preached, and we packed up my car after the service. On the drive home, I couldn't help wishing I could have spent more time with Becky. I was struggling to come to terms with the fact that she was way out of my league.

Thank goodness for moms though. Without my knowing it, Becky's mom had pulled my mom aside after church that day and asked, "Why isn't your son pursuing my daughter? She's interested in him!"

When Mom told me, I almost drove the car off the interstate into the ditch! I was tempted to turn around the car right then and there.

Weeks later, I made the four-hour drive from Sioux Falls to Grand Forks to see her at the University of North Dakota.[6] I was still convinced I didn't have a shot. We hung out over the weekend, and on the way home, I stopped at a truck stop and called my mom. (How did we live without cell phones back then?) I told Mom that I was crazy about Becky but was positive that she'd never date me.

As if I needed any further proof that there is a God, that next week we started dating.

I quickly discovered that I loved being with Becky. More than anything, I loved talking with her. Over time, a shift occurred. Where before I knew about her only from all the folks at church, now I was beginning to know her directly and personally. I knew her heart. Her passions. The things that make her *her.* The more time we spent together, the more we talked and the more I came to know her truly.

A few months later, Becky and I were engaged, and the next summer, married. Years have passed, and just as with my parents, I'm still learning something new about her every day. The more time I'm with her, the more time I spend talking with and listening to her, the more time I'm simply present with her, the more I know her. #boomshakalaka #4kids. I've never loved her more.

———

A few years back, I met someone who's become a dear friend. His name is Roger, and he's ninety-five years young.[7] Here in South Dakota, Roger is a legendary pastor. He's pastored thousands of people, written books, and spoken at conferences all around the world. Roger, however, is quick to remind me that he's "just a recovering sinner in need of Jesus."

Every time Roger and I meet up, God is the center of our conversation. It feels as if it's not two of us talking but rather three, with God himself present.

I'm always quick to ask Roger what he has been learning about life and God, and he typically tells me about God's grace and love, how he's learning to love others as God would want him to. How God is still changing him.

Recently, I visited Roger at his retirement home. We slowly walked to the café, Roger with his walker. We took a break every ten steps or so. He said hello to every passerby. At each walking break, he looked at me and smiled.

As we walked, I asked Roger, "After following Jesus for decades, are you still learning new things about God?"

He responded, "Oh, yes, I feel as though I'm just beginning. Each day when I talk with God, I learn a little more about him than I knew the day before."

Little did I know that would be my last conversation with Roger. He passed away shortly afterward.

Throughout Roger's life, he fell more and more in love with Jesus. He learned more about God, but more importantly, he came to know God through decades of talking with him, through decades of prayer.

When Roger first became a pastor, there was no electronic technology.

Roger didn't learn about God from Google or Facebook. Even with his love for reading, Roger's understanding of God didn't come from books. He learned about God firsthand. Roger learned about God's grace by experiencing it. He learned about God's love by hearing it from the Father in prayer.

I think perhaps this is why Roger's faith was so deep. He learned about God from God. Through years of conversations. There's nothing wrong with reading or studying or Googling, but the best way to know God is to spend time with him. He's the source.

God's love for Roger, God's love for you and me, never fails, increases, or decreases. It is unconditional, limitless. But when we spend time talking with God, we experience that love to a degree we never thought possible.

Like Roger, I am just a recovering sinner in need of Jesus. My relationship with God, specifically my prayer life, is just beginning.

Yet through my conversations with Jesus, I'm falling more in love with him each day.

———

Moments with God are possible, and they exist within each and every day. Beautiful moments. Stressful moments. Broken moments.

When we first wake up and are brushing our teeth. On the treadmill at the gym. As our kids are swinging at the park. At our offices when the to-do list seems to have no end. When we hit rock bottom and feel completely alone.

There are moments to connect with God, moments to experience with God, moments to trust God, moments to come to know him more fully, and moments to talk with God.

My hope is that instead of letting them slip by, we will capture and fully experience these moments with God. I hope we'll grow old with God. That we'll come to know God at the deepest, richest, most intimate levels, spending hours—and days, and weeks, and even years—talking with him. I hope we'll come to share our worries and joys with him. We'll cry with him. Celebrate with him. Sit and be quiet with him.

Talking with God—this is how we fully experience these moments.

Whether you find yourself in the middle of a storm, living in Crazytown, or stuck in mud, I hope you'll talk with God. When you're exhausted or you feel like you're going in circles out on a paddleboat, speak with him.

Jesus, I want to know you.
Jesus I want to be with you.
Jesus, I love you.
Jesus, I want to talk with you for the rest of my life.

Until next time.

Speak, LORD. Your servant is listening.

—1 Samuel 3:9

Before we go, I have one last thing to say.

When we begin to talk to God, there's one thing we can expect: that God will respond to us.

We can expect him to speak.

Something that's important to ask:

Are you listening for him?

Will you hear his voice?

Are you giving him a chance to enter the conversation?

Are you giving him a chance to talk with you?

> I am the good shepherd.
> I know my own sheep and they know me. . . .
> My sheep listen to my voice.
> I know them and they follow me.[1]
> —Jesus

What a friend we have in Jesus,
All our sins and griefs to bear!
What a privilege to carry
Everything to God in prayer!
O what peace we often forfeit,
O what needless pain we bear,
All because we do not carry
Everything to God in prayer!
—"What a Friend We Have in Jesus"
by Joseph Scriven

Thank you.

If you know me, you know that I love to say thank you. I say it often and to many, but the words are true each time I speak them. I have so much and so many reasons to thank God. Many of those reasons are people, so here is my big thank-you.

To the many pastors, leaders, and speakers who have poured into me, spoken at Embrace, and opened doors for me that I couldn't open myself: Roger Spahr, Tyler Reagin, Steve Marytn, Mike Foster, Roger Fredrikson, Jarrid Wilson, James Barnett, Matt Brown, Luke Lezon, Brad Lomenick, Nick Hall, Carlos Whittaker, Annie F. Downs, Bishop Bruce Ough, Jon Weece, David Calhoun, Chris Brown, Matt LeRoy, Jennifer Dukes Lee, Lisa Whittle, Jason Roy, Margaret Feinberg, Adam Hamilton, Craig Groeschel, Brad Montague, Timothy Willard, and Jeff Shinabarger.

To everyone who helped with this book in any way: Seth Haines, Aubrey Wipf, Travis Waltner, Chris Haugan, Sarah Kurtenbach, Sarah Blakely, Angela Tewalt, Katie Daniel, Wendy Tryon, Nathan Schock, Veronyk Dube, Sarah Lavin, Angie Sattler, Bri Cowan, Alli Nix, Adam Burtis, Joe Hubers, Dave DeVries, Derek Harsch, and Kaylyn Deiter.

To Andrew Stoddard, Alex Field, and everyone at WaterBrook Multnomah. I'm truly honored and humbled to work with you.

To Chris Ferebee, for taking a chance on me. I'm beyond grateful to work with the best. Also, you aren't nearly as scary as Tim made you out to be.

To Angela Scheff, for your encouragement, for stretching me and stretching me some more, and for making this book readable. I can't imagine doing this without you. Grateful to consider you a friend.

To Tim Willard. This book happened because of you. Thanks for seeing something in me that I didn't see in myself. Thanks for generously giving me so much—your connections, your advice, and more than anything, your friendship.

To Embrace Church. Rob Kurtenbach, Nikkee Rhody, and the entire staff. To my small group and close friends. To the countless people who call Embrace home. I never thought I could love a church so much. Thanks for allowing me to be your pastor, imperfections and all. Thanks for loving Bec, me, and the kids like you have. I can't wait to see what God will do next!

To Mom and Dad, Jim and Nancy Weber. For doing everything you possibly could to help me come to know Jesus. Thanks for loving each other. For loving us kids. For loving our spouses and kids. For loving Jesus so well.

To Hudson, Wilson, Grayson, and Anderson. I pray you will spend your whole life talking with Jesus. Thanks for teaching me so much about him. Dad loves you so much.

To Bec. Anything I've done has been because of you. Love you.

To *you,* the reader. I'm speechless that you'd read anything I've written. I wish I could grab coffee with you—and maybe someday I will. My only hope for this book is that even one person would begin to talk with God, or talk with God more, because of it. That's my prayer for you.

To you, Jesus. For rescuing me. For loving me. For talking with me.

Field notes.

Everyone else.

1. On this particular occasion, I was at Coffea Downtown. A big thanks to them for the gallons of coffee I drank while writing this book. Honorable mentions go to Queen City Bakery, Pappy's, M. B. Haskett, and Josiah's—you and Jesus made writing this book possible.
2. See Matthew 6:5-15.

1. Found a friend.

1. I have two older brothers. I always tell people I'm a combination of the two. My oldest brother, Hugh, is a genius—like full-ride-to-Harvard genius. He's full of ideas and always dreaming about the next thing. My other brother is Luke. It's hard to miss his beard. He could easily survive in the woods with nothing but his own bare hands. I was the youngest until Becca, my sassy little Korean sister, came along. I love and am so proud of the woman she is. Also, all of my siblings married up! Love you, Amy, Mandy, and Seth.

2. Womb to sixth grade, my family attended American Lutheran Church in Milbank, South Dakota. It was a church filled with great people. Many were relatives. My dad built the blue neon cross that hung on the outside of the building. Also, I have nothing against liturgy and written prayers. I have a deep appreciation for both. Yes, it's easy for them to become a dead ritual, but that's true of any form of worship.

3. Confession: I rarely made it through a full hour of church. Most Sundays, I couldn't sit still that long and ended up talking. And getting in trouble. My dad would march me to the church bathroom to discipline me. It happened so often that I began to think of it as part of the liturgy. Luckily, my dad is one of the nicest guys I know. He would try his best to act upset, give me a warning, and then march me back to our pew. It was like a coach giving a pep talk to his team during halftime of a football game.

4. We moved to Clark, South Dakota, after my last day of sixth grade. Clark is home to the "world famous Mashed Potato Wrestling Contest" and Potato Style Chips. Go Comets!

5. I'm forever grateful for Dr. Aaron Shives, our family doctor and also the person who invited my family to his church. His son Ben, who's also a doctor, is now in my small group.

6. *Different* is the word I use when I'm not really sure what to think. My wife strongly dislikes the word, particularly when I use it to describe something she's wearing or a meal she's prepared.

7. I owe Cornerstone Church in Watertown, South Dakota, so much. It's where I came to know the Lord. It's where I was encouraged to consider being a pastor. It's the church that helped make Embrace, the church I pastor, possible. I'm very thankful for Pastor Roger Spahr and Pat Severson, my youth pastor.

8. Many of the guys and gals who attended this youth group would become the group of people who helped start Embrace in Sioux Falls.

A big shout-out to Tara Melmer, Joe Spahr, Kayla Jones, Scott Binde, Heidi Spahr, Terri Norberg, Eric Knight, and Jeff Lockner.

9. See John 14:6.

10. See John 15:5.

11. John 15:15.

12. See Isaiah 6:2.

13. The British Canadian I'm referring to is the great J. I. Packer. This quote, minus the *eh?,* comes from his classic book *Knowing God* (Downers Grove, IL: InterVarsity, 1973).

14. I loved this car. Four doors. Maroon. Large circle taillights. Almost all of my first conversations with God took place in it. RIP.

15. Fun facts about South Dakota: Bob Barker, Tom Brokaw, and January Jones are from South Dakota. The world's only Corn Palace is in Mitchell, South Dakota. Also, South Dakota has more miles of shoreline than Florida.

2. Easter Bunny.

1. Another year, I got a Salt-N-Pepa CD. Awesome.

2. My favorite Easter childhood memory is of coloring eggs. I didn't like the smell of vinegar though.

3. Ephesians 2:1.

4. While dropping off my kids at school, my first grader randomly said, "Dad, Jesus died and rose from the dead before I was born, right?" And I said, "Yup, he sure did." My son went on to ask, "But, Dad, were you there? Did you see Jesus rise from the dead?" All I could say was, "No, buddy, I didn't. But that would have been cool, huh?" I'm so glad my kid thinks I'm two thousand years old.

5. Ephesians 2:4–5.

6. Ephesians 2:5, NIV.

7. Ephesians 2:4.

8. See Ephesians 3:18–19.

9. For a time, I considered attending Wheaton College. Unfortunately, I haven't been there since that conference back in 1999.

10. I put more miles on my Ford Falcon during those few years than it had seen in the previous forty years. It only had an AM radio in it, and there was an oldies station nearby that came in well.

3. Party of the year!

1. The church I pastor is named after this story. For the first few months after Embrace started, we didn't have a name, so we just called it The New Church. Original, right? Then we made a long list of the names we liked, and Embrace was one of them. One day when I was reading the Bible, I came to Luke 15:20: "He ran to his son, embraced him, and kissed him" (NLT). That same week, someone preached at my seminary's chapel on the story of the prodigal son. Next to the man preaching was a copy of Rembrandt's painting *The Return of the Prodigal Son.* Afterward, I stood and looked at the painting, longing for a church that would resemble it. As of that day, Embrace Church officially had a name.

2. Luke 15:1.

3. See Luke 15:11–32.

4. Luke 15:13, NLT.

5. Luke 15:17, NIV.

6. Luke 15:18.

7. Luke 15:24.

8. Luke 15:25.

9. In college, I used to book punk bands. I had only one show/party get shut down because it was too loud. The band was Dogwood (Tooth & Nail Records).

10. Every July at Embrace, we do a little thing called the Summer Party. Our goal is to get a glimpse of God's party-throwing skills, which gives us a glimpse of his love and grace. The Summer Party typically includes thousands of balloons, countless inflatables, hundreds of baptisms, disco balls, and much more. #partyoftheyear
11. I'm grateful for my in-laws, Randy and Diane Spahr.
12. I already tend to be a helicopter parent. Experiences such as losing my daughter don't help. Pray for me. And her.

4. Short. Simple. Honest.

1. This is the edited version of what my kids pray for. You're welcome for my not including the entire list. Trust me, we've prayed for everything imaginable.
2. Four kids! I can't believe it myself. My oldest is kindhearted and is crazy about Pokémon. His name is Hudson Ray. My second is a gift from God to our family. He's our wild Ethiopian named Wilson Moses. Third is my little princess. She's beautiful inside and out. Her name is Grayson Marie. Our fourth is the surprise. I didn't know it, but our family wasn't complete without the addition of Anderson Adam.
3. Matthew 18:1.
4. See Matthew 18:2–3.
5. Deep thinker and country singer Alison Krauss once sang, "You say it best when you say nothing at all." ("When You Say Nothing at All," written by Paul Overstreet and Don Schlitz, copyright © Paul. L. Overstreet and Scarlet Moon Records.) At times this is the key to having a good marriage. Particularly during an argument. #freemarriageadvice
6. See Matthew 6:5.
7. Psalm 139:4, NIV.

5. Crazytown.

1. You won't find Crazytown on a map. But through a simple search of Google Maps, I discovered that there is a place called Crazytown Live in Pittsburg. That's Pittsburg, Kansas. I have no idea what they do there, but it sounds fun. Or something.

2. I attended Augustana College—now Augustana University—a small Division II school in Sioux Falls. I graduated with a business degree. Those were some of the best years of my life, and I'm still not sure how I graduated, but I did. Go, Augie, go!

3. My wife, Bec, and I got married, then drove to Kentucky the very next day, where I entered Asbury Theological Seminary in Wilmore. I still owe my wife a honeymoon. The three years we lived there were a constant adventure. Being newly married, we discovered a lot about each other before kids showed up. We had a ball. Considering seminary? Go to Asbury!

4. Bill Berry, Michael Mills, Michael Stipe, Peter Buck. "It's the End of the World as We Know It (And I Feel Fine)," copyright © 1987 Warner/Chappell Music, Inc.

5. Come find me. Like me. Follow me. I'd love to connect with you. And then turn off your cell phone more often. Trust me, it is possible to shut off your phone. I've done it. Unplug often.

6. Our dog, Daisy, is a Poochin.

7. Sadly, we recently lost one of our chickens and are down to three. A neighbor's Siamese cat killed Mocha. She lived a good life. RIP, Mocha. #allchickensgotoheaven

8. See 1 Thessalonians 5:14, 15, 16, 17, ESV.

9. Check out Brother Lawrence's book *The Practice of the Presence of God* if you haven't done so. You can finish it in the time it takes to drink a cup of coffee.

10. One of the random things I did a day or two after this was paste a small Bible verse on the door of my dorm room. The next day, I stopped by to meet my next-door neighbor. There was a group of people in this guy's room. The first thing he said to me in front of everyone was, "Hey, what's up, God Squad?" At first I was in complete shock because I couldn't believe he was talking about me. It was like, *God Squad? Adam Weber? What?* All I could think was, *Who goes to college, and instead of becoming a reckless partier, ends up getting labeled "God Squad"? This is so weird!* Usually this kind of thing would have really bothered me, looking like an idiot in front of a group. The crazy thing is, I was strangely okay about it. Honestly, I didn't really care. On a deeper level, there was something solidifying about this moment. It was my moment of saying, "Lord, even if I end up looking like a fool because of you, I'm all in."

11. To quote Miley Cyrus, "We can't stop. And we won't stop." And yes, I did just quote Miley Cyrus. ("We Can't Stop," *Bangerz,* copyright © 2013, RCA Records.)

12. I haven't met a man I respect and love more than my dad. He's taught me what it is to be a man by using more than just words. His life has taught me to be kind and gentle. To work hard. To be honest. To laugh often. He has shown me how to be a husband, a dad, and a follower of Jesus. I hope to be even half the man he is. Any time we talk, my dad ends our conversations with "Love you much, Adam." It never gets old, hearing it.

13. At one point, my dad was the youngest electrician in the state of South Dakota. He was shot twice as a young boy—by his brother! He still has a BB in his hip bone. My dad went to college for one day. #goals. He enrolled but attended only one day of class. I didn't know any of this.

6. Bad driver.

1. I have to say this is one of the best trips our family has ever taken. Becky's parents took her entire side of the family on the trip, and we all have memories that will last a lifetime. My favorite Disney World ride? Peter Pan.
2. Selfie sticks have since been banned, making the Greatest Place on Earth a bit greater.
3. This kid shouldn't be allowed to have a driver's license until he's thirty.
4. Matthew 7:7, 8, 11.
5. Garth Brooks, "Unanswered Prayers," *No Fences,* copyright © 1990, Capitol Nashville.
6. Luke 22:42.

7. Marathon.

1. We do have electricity, but we still don't have a Chipotle in South Dakota. Or a Chick-fil-A. Pray for us.
2. Her first marathon was in Brookings, South Dakota.
3. 1 Thessalonians 5:11, ESV.
4. For my fellow word geeks, it's παρακαλέω (parakaleo).
5. I sat on Minnesota Avenue outside Spoke-n-Sport Bikes. Thanks for encouraging me to do so, Chad.
6. I'm always surprised by how well we're connected with others, yet how little we're actually known as people. On a regular basis, I have people tell me that they really don't know anyone. I've been there myself. We can have countless friends on Facebook yet have not one person to cheer us on. Not one person we can call to ask to pray for us. Or vice versa. If you're there right now, here's my challenge: Get connected to a church. Step out of your comfort zone and find a small group or Bible study. Make relationships with others a priority. And never

forget that God is with you! He's for us, not against us. He's cheering us on!

7. It was near Falls Park in Sioux Falls. The namesake of the town. If you're ever coming through Sioux Falls, stopping at Falls Park is a must. It's beautiful. #hellofromsd

8. My prayer notes are where the idea for this book came from. I send prayer notes almost daily.

9. I currently have eight typewriters. Trust me, though, they're all special.

8. You face storms.

1. For the most part, the worst storms we get here in South Dakota are snowstorms. I once got stuck on Interstate 29 during a storm. By the sheer grace of God, I made it to a rest stop, where I sat for hours before I was rescued by the National Guard in one of those snowcat machines. It was embarrassing and awesome in the same moment. When I stepped into the snowcat, the driver turned around and said, "Adam Weber, what are you doing out there?" Let's just say it's a small world, particularly in South Dakota.

2. Mark 4:35–41, NIV.

3. If you've considered suicide as an option, please reach out and get help. For yourself and those who love you. Talk to a friend. Seek out a Christian counselor. Let someone know that you're struggling.

4. Mark 4:38, NIV.

5. Psalm 18:6.

6. Yup, it's true. My sons can date when they're twenty-five years old. And my daughter is going to become a nun, so, thankfully, I don't need to worry about her.

7. It's a 2009 Chevy Aveo. Four doors. Blue. My tin can on wheels. #baller

8. There's a saying that there are no atheists in foxholes. I think the same has to be true for new dads in delivery rooms. By the way, I am the worst person ever to have in a delivery room. I almost passed out during all three deliveries. When Becky was in labor with Anderson, I started feeling really weird. I remember the doctor telling Becky to say something if at any point her legs felt numb because they shouldn't. All I could think was, *I think my legs are going numb.* About that same time, the doctor said, "Hey, Dad, is everything okay over there?" Because it was my only option as the person who was not in labor, I responded with, "Yup. All is well." I knew for a fact that all was not well. So while I was still sitting down, I decided to start wheeling myself over to the door. "Just going to get some fresh air," I said. I got to the door, opened it, and wheeled myself out. There I was, sitting in the hall, wearing a mask and sweet hairnet, and I'm like, *Thank you, Jesus, for getting me out of there.* I looked up to see a nurse standing three feet away from me. She said, "Pastor Adam, is that you?" For some reason, every time I have an awkward moment, someone is there to recognize me. To sum it up, labor is anything but easy. I've heard the same is true for moms.

9. Mark 4:39, NIV.

10. Mark 4:41, NIV.

11. Matt Redman, "10,000 (Bless the Lord)," *10,000 Reasons,* released July 2011, Kingsway Music.

9. You're discouraged.

1. Andy Dalton is the man! He and T.J. Houshmandzadeh are my favorite Bengals of all time.

2. I've been a die-hard Cincinnati Bengals fan since I was three years old. One of my cousins, Travis Dahle, gave me a Cincinnati Bengals trading

card of Isaac Curtis. I've been a fan ever since. One day we will win a Super Bowl! Hopefully, it'll be before I die. Speaking of football, I pray daily for Pittsburgh Steelers fans. I pray they would repent and start following Jesus.

3. Paraphrase of Psalm 42:1–2, 5, 11.

4. 1 Samuel 13:14, NIV.

5. In a similar way, it's always encouraging to see someone else's kids go completely crazy in the middle of Target. Moms, can I get an amen?

6. See Psalm 42:1–2.

10. You're stuck in the mud.

1. Our cabin is only 625 square feet, but it's my favorite place to be. Whether it's flying kites with the kids, catching a large bass (I mean carp), shooting fireworks, or taking in a sunset, being there is good for the soul.

2. This is a great honor and one of the things I treasure most about my work.

3. Psalm 40:1–3.

4. It may feel weird to talk about Satan, but two of the greatest lies Satan wants us to believe are these:

(1) "Shhh! It's okay, no one will ever find out." Go ahead and look at the website; your wife will never know. Just slide that necklace into your purse; the sales assistant won't see a thing. Just put that money in a different account; the government doesn't need to know anyway. Don't say a word about it; even God doesn't have to know.

(2) "You will never be forgiven." What you've done and are doing is too shameful, too embarrassing, and too terrible. It is impossible to be forgiven, especially by God. There's no coming back after what you've done.

The truth is that a time will come when your actions, habits, and words will be known. Good or bad. They cannot be hidden forever. And they can never be hidden from God. But another truth is that God has already forgiven us of our sins. He does not rank our wrongdoings by order from bad to worst. No matter how big or small a sin is in our eyes, God forgives all. In fact, he already has.

11. You're exhausted.

1. On long road trips when I was a kid, my dad would pull the car over on the side of the road every so often so I could run laps around the car to burn off some extra energy.
2. Grandma Dahle is my mom's mom, and she is my last living grandparent. I love my grandma, but as a kid I was always a bit scared of her. I'm not sure if it was her hugs, her hairy face, or both. Love you, Grandma!
3. Once my dad built a three-wheeler. My sister was in an accident with her Ford Taurus, so my dad took the back end and engine from her car and attached the front end of a motorcycle to it. It was the strangest, goofiest thing I've ever seen on four—I mean, three wheels.
4. Our first get-together as a church was on September 4, 2006. That weekend, I had performed my first wedding, which was my brother's.
5. I attended Asbury Theological Seminary in Wilmore, Kentucky. Wilmore is one of the cutest towns I've ever been in. The place almost feels like a movie set. Bec and I spent three lovely years there. I'm still addicted to sweet tea.
6. September 13, 2009, is a day I will never forget.
7. For four years straight, Embrace was recognized by *Outreach Magazine* as one of the fastest-growing churches in America. In 2015, we

were recognized as the tenth-fastest growing church. I'm still in awe over everything God is doing.

8. Matthew 11:28, NIV.

9. Matthew 11:29, NIV.

10. See Luke 5:16.

11. Are you struggling with burnout yourself? It will take drastic changes to get healthy again. I used to think that if I took just one day off or even a week's vacation that when I got back I would be fine and back to normal again. It wasn't true. To get healthy, it took intentional changes in my life over several months to get back on my feet. If you're struggling, let someone know. Go see a counselor. Make changes and have someone keep you accountable to them.

12. See Exodus 31:17.

13. My nightly walks are usually around downtown Sioux Falls. I live close by, and it's a beautiful area that is undergoing an economic revival. While I walk, I'm usually talking to myself, talking to God, saying hello to passersbys, and listening to Hillsong United. I love my walks.

12. You need an anchor.

1. Our lake place is one of my favorite places to talk with God. It's beautiful. There's no distractions. And there's just something about being near water that makes a person feel closer to God. In our development, none of the lake lots are marked with an address. In place of it, I found an old metal lunch pail, and I put it at the end of our driveway where a mailbox would be. Anytime we have friends out, we just tell them to "look for the lunch pail." Anytime I see a lunch pail, I can't help but think of the lake and talking with God there. Where do you talk with God?

2. Supposedly five people can be on this "boat" at the same time. I wouldn't suggest more than two.
3. If you didn't catch my sarcasm, Tractor Supply is the last place anyone should buy something to navigate on water. If you're looking for chicken feed, go to Tractor Supply. Looking for a good pair of leather gloves, Tractor Supply is the place. Looking for a boat? Go to Long John Silver's before Tractor Supply.
4. The kids and I call the lake "Albert." It's one of the bigger lakes in eastern South Dakota. It's not very busy—or deep, for that matter. I catch walleye and perch in the spring, and carp in the summer.
5. See Hebrews 6:19.
6. I attended Koch Elementary School in Milbank, South Dakota. #IbelieveinMilbank

13. You want to be used by God.

1. I'm thankful to have the best mom a kid could ask for. She was a stay-at-home mom until the age of thirty-four, when she went to college. Mom always dreamed of being a teacher. As young kids (I was ten years old at the time), we thought it was strange that mom was going to college, but now I'm so proud that she did. She finished college and started teaching. A few years later, she went to graduate school. Again, we thought that was strange. Again, I'm so proud of her now. A few days before completing grad school, she was hired as a principal. Some of us are called to be pastors, and others of us are called to be teachers. *Here I am, Lord.*
2. This classic hymn wasn't as classic as I once thought. It was written in 1981 by a Wisconsinite named Dan Schutte. It's based on the words found in Isaiah 6:8.

3. Is there anything better than recess football in elementary school? Nothing beats doing the Ickey Shuffle after scoring a touchdown. Go Bengals!

4. See Hebrews 13:2 and Matthew 10:42.

5. The nursing home Mom and I visited was Whetstone Valley Care Center in Milbank, South Dakota. There was one resident there I'll never forget. I called her the Lady in Pink because she was always dressed in pink clothes. We shared the same birthday.

6. Before being connected to a certain denomination, I'm a follower of Jesus. Although I've never been much of a denomination guy, I'm so grateful for the United Methodist Church.

7. McCabe United Methodist Church

8. I'm thankful for you, Tyler. Thanks for being an encourager, a truth teller, and one of the best friends a person could ask for. Love you, brother.

9. When my mom was pregnant with me, she had a rough pregnancy and made a promise to God that if I was born healthy, she would do everything possible to convince me to become a pastor. She didn't tell me that until I was already in seminary.

10. The fact that you are reading this book is a sign of God's faithfulness. I never wanted to write a book. I never thought I could write a book. After writing it, I never thought anyone would read it. God is faithful.

14. You're trying to extend grace.

1. Best movie ever! Right, Clark?

2. *Christmas Vacation,* directed by Jeremiah S. Chechik, Warner Bros., 1989.

3. When Becky and I were dating, Grace and her husband asked me to stop over at their house one day. They gave me an envelope before I left. Inside was a check for $1,000. They said it was just because. Little did they know that I wanted to buy a ring for Becky so I could propose to her. The next day, I bought her ring.

4. Ephesians 2:8, NIV.

5. John 1:14.

6. Ephesians 3:2.

7. Ephesians 3:7.

8. 1 John 4:19.

9. Colossians 3:13.

10. Sometimes I see grumpy people as a challenge. I think, *I'm just going to annoyingly cover this person with kindness and love until he either starts smiling or dies.* That's probably not a good approach, huh?

15. Capture the moment.

1. It was Evergreen United Methodist Church. The pastor was Randy Spahr, now my father-in-law. Incredibly, he let my twenty-one-year-old self fill in as pastor at his church for a summer.

2. Bec is the single greatest gift I've been given in life. I still can't believe she said yes to marrying me. She knows my faults and imperfections better than anyone. And yet, for some odd reason, she keeps choosing me. She's my best friend. She's the mother to my four kids, our four chickens, and our dog, Daisy. She brings me back to earth whenever I start thinking I'm a big deal. And she's my biggest cheerleader when I'm broken. There is no one else I want to walk through life with. Love you much, Bec. Thanks for always being so good to me.

3. Philippians 3:10, NIV.
4. Once again for my fellow word geeks, the Greek is γινγώσκω (ginosko), which means (1) to learn to know, come to know, get a knowledge of, perceive, feel; (1a) to become known; (2) to know, understand, perceive, have knowledge of; (2a) to understand;
(2b) to know; (3) Jewish idiom for sexual intercourse between a man and a woman; and (4) to become acquainted with, to know. (BibleWorks.com)
5. As a kid, I loved playing NBA Jam. Shawn Kemp was so good. Yes, I call sex "boomshakalaka." I've never really liked the technical terms for things.
6. On my first visit to UND, Becky arranged for me to stay at a college house across from hers. It was a house full of Christian guys. When I arrived, Becky introduced me, and I can't remember a time I've felt more unwelcome by a group of Christians. Did they have something against South Dakotans? As I was trying to fall asleep on the couch that night, one of the guys came down and said, "Just so you know, at one point or another, every guy in this house has wanted to date Becky. Some of us aren't too thrilled that she's thinking about dating you." After that first weekend, these guys became my friends and took me in on each visit to Grand Forks.
7. Roger is truly one of the most amazing people I've known. When we go out to eat, it seems like everyone comes by and says hello. CEOs, city leaders, alcoholics, other pastors and priests, they all stop by to greet Roger. Before ordering, Roger asks the server her name, asks about her story, and offers to pray for her. Roger is also the one who helped me come up with the title of this book. As I was walking toward the door at the end of one of our visits, I asked, "Roger, how would you explain prayer?"

Without skipping a beat, he said, "Talking with God." He smiled and I left.

Until next time.

1. John 10:14, 27.

About Adam.

I like typewriters, drive a Rambler, cheer for the Cincinnati Bengals, and have four chickens. Fun fact: I once made the worldwide news (from the UK, to Pakistan, to Australia) when a turkey vulture fell out of the sky and onto my back porch during an ice storm. Google it. I'm married to my beautiful wife, Becky, and we have four kids: Hudson, Wilson, Grayson, and Anderson. Find out more at adamweber.com.

embrace
C H U R C H

ONLINE   CAMPUS

Join us for worship every hour, on the hour.
iamembrace.com/online